THE CREATIVE EDGE

THE CREATIVE EDGE

Emerging Individualism in Japan

Kuniko Miyanaga

With a Foreword by
Peter L. Berger

Transaction Publishers
New Brunswick (U.S.A.) and London (U.K.)

Copyright © 1991 by Transaction Publishers,
New Brunswick, New Jersey 08903

Library of Congress Catalog Number: 90-49774
ISBN: 0-88738-407-2
Printed in the United States of America

Library of Congress Cataloging-in-Publication Data
Miyanaga, Kuniko, 1945–
   The creative edge : emerging individualism in Japan / Kuniko
Miyanaga : with a foreword by Peter L. Berger.
      p.   cm.
   Includes bibliographical references (p.   ).
   ISBN 0-88738-407-2
   1. Individualism—Japan. 2. Technology—Social aspects—Japan.
I. Title.
HM136.M591   1991
302.5'4'0952—dc20   90-49774
                                                              CIP

To my late parents

Contents

Foreword

Japan has been looming over the American imagination for well over a decade now—as a dramatic spectacle, as an intellectual puzzle, as an ideal to be emulated, as a challenge, and possibly as a threat. This fascination with Japan is likely to increase even further in the coming decade, as Japanese economic power continues to grow (a near-certainty) and as political worries are replaced by economic worries in the foreign relations of the United States (hardly a certainty, but a distinct possibility). Needless to say, America has loomed just as large in the Japanese imagination, with even greater ambiguities, some going back to the earliest encounters between Japan and the West. There are elements of high comedy in the resultant game of mirrors. Mutual perceptions, of course, keep changing. Especially in America, where academic careers are made by one cohort of aspiring experts shooting the theories of the preceding cohort out of the water (an exotic ritual of symbolic parricide that yet awaits its ethnographer, perhaps a Japanese one, since Japanese culture gives one a very fine sensitivity to ritual), there has been a lot of such change.

For a while there was the prevailing view of "Japan, Inc.," a society organized with incredible efficiency for economic super-performance under the aegis of near-infallible government agencies (notably, of course, the famous or notorious MITI—Ministry of International Trade and Industry). Then came second thoughts about this view among American Japanologists: books and articles that pointed to the conflicts and the costs of the Japanese system, that debunked MITI and the role of government in general, and that even argued that there were built-in weaknesses in the Japanese way of doing things. Today's politicians tend to have read (or had summaries read to of) books by yesterday's academics, so that we still have ringing calls for an American "industrial policy" more or less modeled on what Japan was thought to be like. But, as is pointed out by analysts of the times on every possible occasion, we live in an age of instant global communication: The experts are read by many of the people about whom their expertise is assumed, and this is not without effect on these people. Thus there is some reason to think that some Japanese have come to believe what foreign experts have written about them—and not only have they believed it, but they have modified their behavior according to it. In any case, Americans and Japanese (arguably the most introspective nations in the contemporary world) have not only been interpreting and reinterpreting each other, but have greatly worried about these reciprocal interpretations (they are also two nations of obsessive worriers).

No more can be said here about the ever-changing Japanese vision of America. The American vision of Japan has tended to hinge, in large measure, on the interpretation of the alleged Japanese collectivism—or "groupism," as the relevant Japanese term is usually translated. Compared with Western cultures, the Japanese, in this view, are highly collectivistic or group-oriented, by the same token anti-individualistic. This foreign interpretation of Japanese culture neatly tallies with one particular strand of Japanese self-interpretation, usually in the context of a larger argument as to the uniqueness of Japanese culture. Both American and Japanese interpreters have differed in their evaluation of this alleged "groupism": Some regard it as a great strength (healthy Japanese community versus decadent, atomizing, selfish American individualism), others as a source of weakness (Japanese robot-like conformists against the innovative creativity of American individualists). It follows that, as some American Japan-experts have been telling their compatriots to emulate Japan, Japanese Americanists have urged *their* compatriots to learn from America. Perhaps the high point of this comedy of national masochisms in interaction has been in the area of education: American educators became near-berserk in their admiration of the Japanese educational system at precisely the moment when the criticisms of the same system in Japan came to a crescendo. But then, of course, there is another view of Japan, one that de-emphasizes its "groupy" character. And here one finds those interpreters who see Japan and the West on converging paths, two advanced industrial societies (or post-industrial societies, if one prefers) who will inevitably come to resemble each other, with Western individualism driving out or at least greatly modifying Japanese collectivism. Needless to add, this putative Westernization is looked upon as bad news by some, as good news by others.

There are theoretical as well as political prejudices that push people into the view that each culture is not only unique but unchangingly so (what I like to call the ancient curse theory of history) and other people into viewing the modern age as a gigantic process of homogenization (the cosmic Osterizer theory, if you like). Nevertheless, prejudices apart, there are empirical grounds for taking one or the other view about Japan. There is good evidence to the effect that Japan is a highly distinctive society and that an important part of this distinctiveness is a great capacity for group loyalty and cooperation, and, ipso facto, strong pressures to subordinate individual aspirations to the needs of the group. Indeed, one can argue plausibly that Japan's great cultural achievement in its modern period, first undertaken during the Meiji period and then taken up again powerfully after World War II, has been to transform a feudal-military ethos of group solidarity into an ideology of great effectiveness in modern economic organizations. But there is also good evidence that Japanese culture is changing. Especially among the young there are data showing attitudes and behavior that, by any reasonable measure, must be called more individualistic and less "groupy." There are also data indicating that this is not just a youth phenomenon but rather that it persists into middle age. Empirical evidence does not always point toward a middle ground between competing theories; in this case, I believe, it does. Japan will continue to be a very distinctive society, unlikely to resemble individualistic America in the foreseeable future; at the same time, there are some changes in Japanese society that do indeed converge toward certain American patterns, of which individualism is one. In other words, as so often, it is a matter of degree and not an either/or proposition.

If that is the way to look at it, then a crucial question becomes one of sectors: Which sectors of Japanese societies are changing in a more individualistic direction, and which are not (or at least are changing less)?

If the question is phrased in this manner, Kuniko Miyanaga's book provides a necessarily tentative but highly interesting answer. It is contained in her analysis of two sectors of Japanese society which she calls "mainstream" and "periphery." The mainstream is precisely the world of "Japan, Inc.," the world of the large corporations, which continues to dominate both economically and ideologically. It is also the world of "groupism." At no time did this sector contain the entire society. There was always an "other Japan," on the periphery, and its world was more tumultuous, more individualistic. But, or so Miyanaga argues, this periphery has recently become much more important economically. In such areas as the fashion industry, in high technology and in venture-capital firms, individualists who would never make it with Hitachi or Toyota suddenly find themselves with very lucrative economic opportunities. Among them, very significantly, are a growing number of women. Now, it is important to stress that Miyanaga is not arguing that there were no individualists in Japan before, but rather that these people, who before could just try to survive, now find that they can make out very well and often more rapidly than within the old hierarchies.

Miyanaga also contends that there is now a mutual influence (she calls it a "dialectic") between these two sectors. As enterprises on the periphery grow larger and more successful, they feel the pull of the old ideology. Perhaps every little entrepreneur in Japan dreams, at least occasionally, of being a Toyota one day. But the periphery influences the mainstream, despite its culturally less prestigious place. It does so for the simplest of reasons: Mainstream organizations have discovered that they need the "creative edge" that comes from the periphery. They may even have discovered that they need individualists. Thus Miyanaga's book presents an original and nuanced contribution to a very important debate over the future of the Japanese economy. It is a debate of great fascination for social scientists. It also has far-reaching practical implications.

The research that led to this book was supported by the Institute for the Study of Economic Culture (ISEC) at Boston University, a research center exploring the relation between economic and socio-cultural change. This project was part of a much larger program of research into changing corporate cultures which, at the time of writing, includes projects in the United States, Western Europe, India, and the newly industrialized countries of East Asia.

The support for Miyanaga's project came from grants by the John M. Olin and the Sarah Scaife foundations. I would like to take this occasion for thanking them once again for their generous funding of ISEC's program. I also want to thank Jane Uscilka, whom ISEC retained in an editorial capacity in preparing the manuscript for publication; she performed this task with unusual competence, care and tact. Finally I want to express my appreciation of the encouragement given to this project by Irving Louis Horowitz, who once again has exhibited his truly extraordinary capacity for combining the roles of publisher and intellectual states-man.

PETER L. BERGER

Director, Institute for the Study of Economic Culture, Boston University

Preface

This book grew out of a conviction that if there ever were to be a time when individualism could spread actively in Japan, it would be now. My research not only confirmed my personal feeling, which had, from the viewpoint of social science, remained only hypothetical for a long time; it also led to the discovery that individualism is flourishing in entrepreneurship. It is invigorating an already vital Japan, and its continued growth will be ensured by what I call the "structural pluralism" in Japanese society.

I interviewed many Japanese who thought of themselves as individualists and who believe, as I do, that Japan is not a culturally simple and homogeneous nation whose citizens are all born with an innate Japanese-ness–the word indicates an essence of collectivity that makes a person or a thing profoundly Japanese. Such words as *nihon-teki* (Japan-like) and *nihon-jin* (a Japanese) are commonly applied to signify the essence. Hence, "being a Japanese" is synonymous with carrying the essence of Japanese collectivity. The opinion leaders of the modern culture of technology promote this viewpoint by applying theories and methods in social science, ignoring other options available in Japanese society. Those I interviewed expressed frustration at this circumstance that has excessively impressed the West with the role of collectivity in Japan. I was introduced to a number of other individualists through the "horizontal" networks of relationships (about which I write in chapter 3) that exist in Japan. These networks are endless, although hidden, like secret trails in a deep forest.

The importance placed upon group collectivity and nationalism in Japan has forced individualism to be repressed and concealed. Traditionally, it has been a quiet subculture on the periphery of society, finding expression primarily in religion and the arts, practiced by society's "dropouts," while the majority of the population remained group-oriented. In other words, individualism has been viewed as deviant by the mainstream, yet it has performed an essential function on the periphery. Traditionally, individualism has been viewed as a passive choice to follow a deviant lifestyle, withdrawing from the mainstream into a small compartment on the periphery. It created a social option but did not lead to social change. Instead, it solidified a given social structure by discharging the deviant elements from the mainstream.

This traditional separation and juxtaposition between groupism and individualism has continued into the present. Since 1945, the modern Japanese culture of technology has developed based on a hierarchical network of human relationships (the "vertical principle") in groups. In this social context, the collectivity of the Japanese has been given a special name, "groupism," indicating that Japanese collectivity displays a particular structure which ensures group loyalty and the work ethic. With further economic growth since the 1960s, some individualists on the periphery of the Japanese economy have gained a position strong enough to enable them to interact with the mainstream without losing their independence. The number of such entrepreneurs who wish to remain on the periphery has added new momentum to Japan's development.

Against the active attempts among entrepreneurs and also against the groupism of the modern culture of technology, a new form of passive individualism has become popular, especially among the younger generation, that is, privatization of groups and family-centrism. These individuals, basically, have withdrawn from the task group. Their kind of withdrawal has not led to social change, but it has created a source of silent support for more active individualists by accentuating the existence of structural pluralism. The failure of the active individualist movement has encouraged the youth generally to lean in the direction of forms of passive individualism; the emphasis of their social orientation has shifted from the work ethic to family life, and from loyalty to the task group to that of their own private groups. The failure of Japanese youth to contribute to the integration of active individualism into the mainstream attests to the great strength groupism still has in Japan. At the same time it reveals, ironically, the potential importance that active, peripheral individualism in entrepreneurship has for the future social and economic development of Japan as a continuing antithesis to the dominant groupist culture.

In this book, I have tried to put these changes into perspective by identifying two major interactions between cultures. The first is the formation of the modern culture of technology. It is viewed here as a synthesis between traditional values and a modern economy, as well as between Japanese tradition and the pressures of Westernization, since the modern economy has been adopted from the West. A second, concurrent interaction is now emerging between the modern culture of technology as the economic mainstream (the groupist culture) and the periphery (the individualist culture). Although not unaffected by influences from other societies, the contemporary interaction between Japan's two cultures has arisen primarily from sources within the structure of Japanese society itself. Within this social context, it is significant that subcultures, traditionally juxtaposed to the mainstream, are now interacting dynamically with elements of the mainstream, generating new momentum for the further development of Japanese society.

Acknowledgments

The writing of this book was made possible by the sponsorship of the Institute for the Study of Economic Culture at Boston University and its director, Dr. Peter Berger. My original research was conducted mainly in Tokyo with the financial support of the Institute. I met Dr. Berger at an international conference on religion and science held in Tokyo. After my presentation, Dr. Berger, a distinguished guest at the conference, offered me the Institute's sponsorship for writing a book on individualism in Japan, based on my own research, as part of the Institute's project on Asian development. He read my manuscript several times and gave me advice throughout its writing. I am more than grateful to him. The book was completed under the academic sponsorship of the Philosophy of Education Center at Harvard University and Professors Israel Scheffler and Vernon Howard, the Center's co-directors.

I must give special thanks to the people who helped me contact those whom I interviewed for the book: Drs. Michio Nagai, former minister of education, and Kinhide Mushakoji, former vice president of the United Nations University; Mrs. Kazuo Tsushima, former senior officer of the United Nations University, and Koji Kobayashi, chairman of Nippon Electric Company. I feel greatly indebted to all the people I interviewed.

I also thank the people in business who helped me understand some essential aspects of corporate transactions: Professor Ron Nahser of Du Paul University (also president of Franc Nahser

Advertisement, Inc.), and Professors Robert Rosane (former vice president of ALCAN) and Roger Putzel of St. Michael's College.

I am particularly grateful to a number of people who advised me in articulating my thoughts in English, my second language, including my copy editors. Among them, I greatly owe Jane Uscilka, who helped me express my thoughts in English, my second language. She helped me to make my writing in English take on the same tone my writing in Japanese has; I was lucky to be able to work with her. I am also grateful to my friends in America and Japan who provided me with the psychological support to write this book, and to my family who allowed me to concentrate on the writing of the book.

1

Individualism and Groupism

The Formation of a Modern Culture of Technology

From the so-called period of Japan's high economic growth (1955–1974) to the present, the goal of groupism has been to encourage and promote, against individualism, the "modern culture of technology," assigning Japan a leadership role in Asia.

Until the 1960s, modernization in Asia meant Westernization,[1] a view held by the majority of Japanese. To them, the advent of modernization appeared as a total acceptance of Western civilization, the relinquishing of indigenous Asian cultures, including the Japanese culture, or as a total shift from indigenous culture to Western civilization. Segments of society excluded from the shift were considered failures. Stage theories in development were imported to organize and accelerate this process, not only by Western-educated intellectuals but also through foreign aid and advisers from developed Western countries.

The change in Asian societies was chiefly motivated by the economic benefits they stood to gain, in particular the creation of a high-quality labor market. In this area, Japan took an early lead. At the same time, this change raised difficult social and cultural problems relating to class-status orientations, rural-urban relations, interpersonal relationships, the family system, and the position of women. Because the basic motivation for change was economic, it was felt by many that the aim of the Western challenge was to demoralize people by driving them into material pursuits that

1

disclaimed indigenous moral values. In this context, a fear of individualism emerged, and individualism has become synonymous with egocentrism or social apathy.

In this book, social changes will not be viewed as a simple shift from stage A to stage B, that is, from traditional to Western culture, but rather as a combination of the two cultures. In the process of modernization, tradition has been well maintained, at the same time that Western technology has been adopted successfully. In the late 1980s, it became increasingly clear that tradition and Westernization have been blended into a new socio-economic reality which may be referred to as the modern culture of technology in Japan. The significance of this outcome is that the original two elements—tradition and modernization—have yielded a whole greater than the sum of its parts, exhibiting characteristics that are possessed by neither of the original elements. Putting it in Hegelian terms, the economic culture of Japan is a synthesis between the Japanese tradition as thesis and Westernization as antithesis. This is the real uniqueness of today's Japanese culture of technology, a somewhat different view from the Japanese perception of their own uniqueness: the Japanese tend to conclude that their success is a result of their defense of traditional values. Instead of achieving stage B, they insisted on staying at stage A, in response to Western pressures. This has already become a source of national pride.

There is an essential difference between the Japanese dialectical development under Westernization and the European case, the latter having been presented by Hegel as a model for social change. In the European version, the dialectical process emerged from the indigenous culture itself; it is possible that it may have evolved from conflicts between Christian elements and Hellenistic influences. It is viewed as an internal process within a given civilization, where a synthesis becomes a thesis from which various antitheses emerge, creating future dialectical development.

In contrast to the European example, Westernization in Japan clearly has been imposed by external force. Western scientific, technological, and material culture was alien to nineteenth-century Japan. The Western paradigm was enforced over and against Japanese tradition. Although the Japanese later acknowledged some elements in common with their tradition and Western culture, such elements do not stand to refute either the essential differences between Japanese tradition and Western culture or the fact that the introduction of Western concepts generated a dialectical process that led to the formation of a new Japanese economic culture, characterized by the emergence of technocrats.

It must be noted that the dialectical perspective of the modernization process in the non-Western world is one commonly and strongly held by other social scientists in Asia. I have met many who share such notions through the scholarly network of the United Nations University. Kyong-Dong Kim, a prominent sociologist in Korea, has remarked, "Whether you like it or not, modernization of latecomer societies should be seen as a dialectical process of international acculturation and indigenous adaption."[2]

Kim's observation indicates that the historical process experienced in Japan is not unique but universal to the non-Western world. There is economic evidence: NICs (Newly Industrialized Countries, meaning Korea, Taiwan, Singapore, and Hong Kong) are catching up to Japan, and even ASEAN (Association of South East Asian nations: Thailand, Indonesia, Malaysia, the Philippines, Singapore, and Brunei) countries are catching up to the NICs.[3] Asia is moving and developing in the same direction as Japan, and the process is perceived as a dialectical one by many scholars.

To date, this perception of development has not been articulated as a dialectical theory, perhaps because the term "dialectic" seems out of date. To most Americans, it is a term that is part of Marxist ideology, and to many Marxists, unless it is applied to the overthrow of the bourgeoisie by the working class, it is a false concept. Perhaps here *dialectic* should be understood in its original Greek sense—a dialogue, from which unexpected results emerge. In this book the term will appear to indicate a dialogue between cultures or subcultures, through their bearers, directed toward the creation of new cultures. This wider interpretation is necessary in order to understand the process in Asia where change is both cumulative and innovative.

Individualism in Transformation

A dialectical process of modernization in Asia is evident in the emerging individualism in today's Japan. Under the influence of

Westernization, it represents a new development in the individualism that has traditionally existed in Japan. Today, individualism in Japan has taken on new forms of expression, historically and culturally distinct from individualism as it exists in the West.

Although rarely mentioned in literature about Japan, "dropping out" of established groups for the purpose of self-realization, a form of "passive individualism," has been a long-standing tradition. Buddhism, the official religion of the premodern age, often promotes resignation from social achievement. Buddhism's supreme achievement is oneness with nature, and its prophesy is not commonly expressed socially. This characterization may best apply to Zen Buddhism, the religion of the ruling class in the premodern age. The ruling class learned spontaneity with nature and with the self, and it withdrew from the earthly desire for long life to become masters of the martial arts. At the same time, this withdrawal made them detached from the given social system and enabled them to stand above it. However, to function socially, they adopted Confucianism, the ethical and political philosophy of the fifth century B.C., from China, which built the state's foundation on loyalty toward kin, particularly on filial piety. Thus, in Japan, Confucianism and Buddhism coexisted in a delicate internal balance. It was understood that sometimes that balance was lost, and there were those who withdrew from the hierarchy of social achievement. Such a person became a "drop-out," for example a Buddhist monk, or in extreme cases, dropped out of life by the socially accepted route of suicide. Although, in practice, suicide and dropping out are very different forms of individual expression, in this context there is an ideological continuity between them.

Another common secular form of "dropping out" in Japan was involvement in the arts. Religion and art provided the drop-out with a moral structure and a concrete method of self-realization through which identity crises could be overcome. The drop-out lives for his own values and quality of life, not for social success or prestige attached only to the establishment. However, this situation does not rule out the position of religion and the arts as integral parts of the establishment. A Buddhist priest or an artist could achieve prestige and even wealth by joining the establishment. This is an example of one of the many double definitions commonly found in

Japanese society that provide social options. A person could either invest his ability in the establishment or simply live by art or by religion for its own end. It is clear that in this social dynamic, prestige, a quality of group identity, could not be obtained outside of the establishment. Thus prestige, not wealth, was the most essential component of elite membership.

The expression of individualism by dropping out is not unique to Japan in the non-Western cultures. The anthropologist Kenelm Burridge, in his ambitious book *Someone No One* (1979), argues that individualism is more prevalent outside of Western culture than has been understood. Its lack of recognition outside of the West is due to the fact that individualists in non-Western societies are assigned to prescribed social positions on the periphery of the community; they are permitted to develop lifestyles which express different qualities and values, but socially they are not allowed to merge with "normal" people. In his comparative analysis, Burridge points out that the role of individualism as a leading force for social change is a tenet of capitalism, practiced mainly within the European venue until the age of colonialism. In non-Western cultures, individualists were harmlessly compartmentalized on the periphery of society. Some examples of such individualists in different cultures are those who have played the roles of shaman in Siberian and Eskimo culture; the Nuer Leopard-Skin Chief in the Nile River region; the Melanasian sorcerer in the South Pacific; and the Hindu *guru*. Burridge's argument suggests that with colonial expansion, Western-style individualism was exported to non-Western societies, creating a new impetus as two distinct kinds of individualism conjoined.

Traditional Japanese individualism has found a new form of expression in the modern economy. It is not a simple shift from traditional to Western. Individualists are still considered peripheral, unlike the Western case, due to the dominance of groupism in the mainstream of Japanese society. However, individualists in the fashion industry, for example, are no longer "drop-out" artists or religious individuals encapsulated in compartments estranged from the mainstream. Before their ascendency during the period of high economic growth, as Burridge suggests, they represented cultural options and even became exemplars of an "asocial" lifestyle, a counterimage to what "social" life should be. The relationship between drop-out individualists and the "normal" population was one of harmonious and detached coexistence. But a primary difference today is that, unlike the artists in premodern times, artists and designers know that business can be made out of art. Of course there is variance among individual artists; some are more or less commercially oriented than others. But the point is that they are not artists who have simply withdrawn to prescribed positions on the periphery of society. They are artists by choice, and the flourishing Japanese economy has given them the advantage of being able to remain on the periphery, while advancing economically. The following case study, about the early years in the life of Kansai Yamamoto, one of many I conducted, is a good example.

A Case Study

Kansai Yamamoto, a leading fashion designer, told me that for him fashion design is a self-realization, not simply designing others' appearances. His biography is a coming-of-age tale of self-realization during Japan's age of economic success and speaks for the popular passions of the times:

> The reason I chose to be a fashion designer was that designing clothes was the quickest and the most appropriate way to express myself. This was an almost totally intuitive choice. As I let my impulse flow out of my whole being, I found myself as a fashion designer. When I reflect on the process of becoming a designer, I feel I was moved by some invisible force.[4]

It would not be a mistake to assume that the "invisible force" was a desire for self-expression, shared by many in Japanese society at the time. Yamamoto continued, "I have always challenged myself to be new. I have concentrated my senses on the 'antenna' through which I have felt and captured how and where the age has been moving."[5]

Yamamoto was born in 1944, one year before the end of World War II. His father was a tailor. He entered Nippon University, majoring in English literature, but in 1964, when he was twenty years old, he decided to leave school and consequently relinquished the possibility of a professional position in an established firm. He gave up opportunities for security and prestige but began his route toward the achievement of his own goal: that of self-expression. From the point of view of the establishment at that time, fashion was a trivial pursuit. He entered Junko Koshino's well-known workshop as a stitcher, receiving a minimum salary, barely enough for him to live on. Average wages in Japan were low in general. Japanese textile products were sold in the lower-quality American markets. American buyers were generally critical of Japanese fashion designers, noting the lack of Western appeal in the clothes coming out of Japan. However, even then designers such as Koshino, Hanae Mori, Issei Miyake, and others were preparing to join the top ranks of the international market; taking advantage of their unfamiliarity with Western designs, they added exotic charm to them. Yamamoto was one of many who struggled to keep pace with this group, which synthesized Japanese and Western traditions using its own innovations.

In 1967, in the midst of high economic growth in Japan, Yamamoto received the grand prize in a major designing contest in Japan and became recognized as a professional. In 1971, he established his own small company. He became known as an avant-garde designer. He says:

> Gradually, I was building up my own fashion. I disliked and resisted square clothes whose quality was in their expensive material and good sewing. The popular color for them was already established and beyond my reach. I wished to capture the hearts of the people who wore my clothes. I tried to depend on their feelings. Expression of individuality was the key point. My fashion was going ahead of the time. But, at the same time, it was American. I had to override this. This was a huge wall.[6]

In 1974, Japan was struck by the energy crisis. It was the end of the age of great economic growth, and the beginning of the slow-down economy. Yamamoto's reputation suffered damage after he staged a Paris fashion show that was successful from an artistic point of view, but proved to be a failed investment. He could not easily recover the losses. Workers left his company, and he lost friends. Working with the few people remaining in his firm, he reached the conviction that successful creativity and economic entrepreneurship must be achieved together:

Creation and business. Presenting these two together will give me a strong position. The fashion designers used to be able to impress people through their artistic creation. But now only by handling these two together can they appeal more strongly to people. In the creation of clothes, I can impress them with my total self.[7]

What is most illuminating about Yamamoto is that he began his business and his artistic career out of a passion for self-realization, not out of a passion for enterprise. He went into business for himself because he could not find his way in the mainstream. Young Yamamoto is only one of many in Japan who are content to maintain a modest standard of living in order to achieve personal goals in their lives. Cafés, restaurants, and small shops are owned by people whose goals do not include prestige or wealth. Toys and crafts are designed by such people, making Japanese life more richly colored with their art. As more money flowed out of the mainstream in the 1960s and 1970s, the number of small businesses increased enough to compete on a financial scale roughly equal to that of Japan's automobile industry. But small businesses had to wait until the 1980s for even greater financial success.

Hard-Working Older Generations

The generation before Yamamoto's, those born prior to the end of World War II (the "pre-war generation") initiated the age of high economic growth, and their self-motivation is still sustaining Japan's economic success. They are the generation who suffered from shortages of food and staples during and after the war, who even now are haunted by the memory of starvation. Some of them say that Japan was not defeated by the United States Army but its own starvation, an attitude comparable to the "Depression mentality" of some older Americans. It is difficult for the youth to understand the older generation. A Japanese newspaper cartoon makes this point: the cartoon features a man of the older generation first eating the rice grains sticking to the lid of his lunchbox, because the rice is imbued with an almost spiritual value and should not be wasted. He carefully picks up each grain. Then, he stops eating without finishing all of the rice, saying that he does not want to get fat. Yamamoto's "post-war generation," which also experienced undernourishment, recalls the time when local goods were still extremely limited and of poor quality, but the overwhelming prosperity of America was indicated in every bit of the imported products.

Yukiko Hanai, whom I also interviewed, is one of the most successful fashion designers in Tokyo. She spent her childhood in post-war Japan. She grew up in a small town, fantasizing over Western culture. "I went to see almost all the Western films that came to my town," she recalled, "but, every time I came back from the movie theater, I found myself in a bad mood." When her mother asked why, she answered that in the film the West was not "correctly" reflecting her own image of what it was like. "I could not stand the gap," she said, with a self-knowing smile. So, she realized her "correct" image of the West in the clothes she created when she became a fashion designer. From a psychological perspective, she felt compelled to become a designer to correct the flaws in their image created by Westerners themselves.

While a little girl was fantasizing about dresses, many boys were dreaming of automobiles. It was no accident that the fashion and automobile industries both grew rapidly between 1955 and 1974. For the older generation, cars were not simply conveniences; they embodied a kind of perfection. Thus, during the serious competition between American and Japanese car manufacturers, Japanese consumers rejected American cars because of "pin holes," tiny spots left by air bubbles in the paint commonly used then. The rejection offended the Americans, who considered it an excuse on Japan's part to close the Japanese market against American cars. A more accurate reading may be that Japanese consumers were not simply demanding a sufficient product but a flawless one. Although the tiny defects in the American cars were almost invisible, the old Chinese saying, "A slight scratch stands out more on a perfect jade," reflects the Japanese perspective.[8]

Strange Symptoms in a New Generation

Compared to the hard-working older generation, the new generation appears to be spoiled by material prosperity. From 1985 to 1988, the youth were known as *shin jinrui* ("New Men" or mutants). They no longer acknowledged the vast difference between traditional Japanese and Western culture that had been a central theme in the lives of their elders. Those elders had labeled each other with terms such as "old-fashioned" (meaning traditional) or "updated" (meaning Westernized or Americanized). To the older generation, the gap between tradition and Westernization was unquestionable. Slang idioms to indicate such differences emerged, but they have not lasted.

Among the older generation, Jean-Paul Sartre had been extremely popular. A series of his works translated from the French was prominently displayed in every bookstore. His philosophy suggested to those Japanese who felt lost between tradition and Westernization that continuity between the past and the future is an act of social creation, brought about by human efforts. Many intellectuals attempted to create a synthesis between the past and the future, based on interpretations of Sartre's thought. By the 1980s, however, the youth no longer recognized such a gap between tradition and Westernization. They were not concerned with origins. Sartrean existential themes held no appeal; fashion thrived, capturing the synthesis between tradition and Westernization in fragmented visual messages.

A foreign concept may be so quickly assimilated by a population that it believes the concept has always been a part of its own culture. This point was brought home to me when I recently taught a class of female students at Tokyo Women's College. When I mentioned that Japanese democracy had been adopted from Western and American democratic systems, nearly every student objected, insisting that Japan always had been democratic. When I later explained that the notions of equality under the law and the "legal person" were basic to democracy, the students had to admit that these concepts had hardly existed in Japan. Yet it had required a conscious search by the students for the demarcation between tradition and Westernization in their culture before they could identify it.

The older generation was at first puzzled by the youth whose behavior no longer fit into the old matrix of "traditional" and "Western." The gap that had been created between these poles was diminishing among the youth. In the older generation's view, the youth no longer had a gap to fill. It had provided the impetus for the older generation in the construction of its own economic culture, a fulfillment of physical and psychological needs. The loss of such impetus among the youth may have been only indicative of a generation gap, but it did not appear to be an ordinary one. The existing economic culture might have been at a dead end.

The fear of losing the dynamic tension and interaction between tradition and Westernization is related to a conviction among the Japanese that Japan is a homogeneous nation. According to this conviction, if Japanese modernity is a synthesis between tradition and Westernization, the loss of a heterogeneous outside element could lead the whole process into inertia. There would be no further development or social dynamic to drive people to further economic success. Society would deteriorate in economic prosperity in the same way as, the Japanese believe, it has in America. In this social context, individualism is seen as an "American disease" threatening groupism, a necessary evil attached to the American-style democracy which has been in force in Japan since 1945. As the rapid infusion of Westernization wanes in Japan, the Japanese fear that only such negative bequests will remain. The rising crime rate in Japan is feared to be a reflection of America's crime problems, an indicator that the American disease is further corrupting Japan. In order to analyze more deeply the cause of the fear of individualism, the nature of the belief in cultural homogeneity must be further explored.

Cultural Diversity

The notion of the homogeneity of the Japanese nation has not only been perpetuated by the Japanese themselves, it has also become a popular conception in America. A CBS newscast featured a white male business correspondent who answered the question, "Why are the Japanese doing so well economically?" by replying, "In Japan everyone is a Japanese." The answer disturbed a black male news reporter, because it sounded as if some people in America were not American enough, and thus they were responsible for current economic problems. Although I may not be in a position to evaluate American attitudes, I do know, in fact, that there are many Japanese, including individualists, who are considered not Japanese enough, and who are criticized and often discriminated against by those who consider themselves "fully qualified" Japanese.

Japan's Korean and Chinese minorities have been traditionally discriminated against. There is also antagonism between those from the eastern and western regions of Japan; those from the west often complain that they never feel accepted in Tokyo, located in the east. In western Japan, people from the east are referred to as *bando mono,* literally "a person from the east," which carries the derogatory connotation of "uncivilized." In the same way that ethnic background carries associative connotations either positive or negative in America, regional (prefectural) backgrounds are socially significar.t to the Japanese. Most Japanese in social situations speak the standardized versions of Japanese propagated by the centralized education system and the media. This is roughly analogous to the "mid-Atlantic" accent favored by broadcasters in America. However, with intimate friends or those with the same regional or social background, the Japanese may speak in their own dialect or accent, with the assumed risk of alienating those who are unfamiliar with their regionalisms. Common wisdom holds that all Japanese speak two kinds of Japanese, standard Japanese and their own dialects, creating both uniformity and diversity in the same language. Similar variations in many features in Japanese life confuse Americans, who expect clear-cut, consistently delineated social traits in others.

Modernization as Centralization

People who speak two versions of the Japanese language are a result of the historical process of modernization. Before the Meiji Restoration in 1868, premodern Japan was separated into more than one hundred territories ruled by feudal lords. Although the lords traveled periodically between their own territories and Edo, the capital city (now Tokyo), their people were not allowed to leave the territory unless given special permission for reasons such as religious pilgrimages to famous shrines or temples. It has been suggested that the development of local dialects was promoted in order to more easily recognize outsiders stealing into other fiefdoms, including spies, especially from the Shogunate. Social and physical mobility was low. About 85 percent of the total population is estimated to have been peasants and farmers, settled peacefully in their own villages for two-and-a-half centuries. In addition to the strict political separation of the feudal territories, the Japanese geography, 70 percent of which is steep mountains and difficult water passages, made communication difficult. Premodern Japan was characterized by diffusion of power, high security, cultural diversity, low mobility, and the containment of community.

A key goal of the process of modernization was centralization. Political power was consolidated and has continued, through political turmoils, to be centralized. Until the end of World War II, a centralized military power was continually built up; at the end of the war, its size was greatly reduced. The occupying forces then imposed even more strongly a unified educational system in order to promote democracy. This educational system is now highly refined and has been fortified by economic growth; it has created a sense of homogeneity based on the common educational background of all members of society. The first nine years of education are essentially free in the public system, and as a result, there is virtually one hundred percent literacy. Legally, parents have no right to refuse to allow the education of their children by the government, while the government has no right to deny education to children.

Such centralization of power has its drawbacks. As a personal illustration, I recall visiting my relative's family in Niigata Prefecture; my aunt complained that the content of the workbook her grandson was studying was not accurate. The book asked when the nightingale would begin to sing. She had told her grandson, "in May." The following day, he came home from school quite upset, saying that the correct answer was "March." My aunt observed, "It might start singing in March in Tokyo, where the authors of the workbook must live, but here it does not start until May. It is colder here. Besides, the weather is different every year. Sometimes the bird starts earlier, and sometimes later."

Such inconsistencies come up constantly, and the Japanese must adjust accordingly. Sharing the same basic knowledge creates a strong feeling of homogeneity, but it is at the risk of sacrificing local realities and treating them as "errors." The unity of the Japanese as a nation is synonymous with homogeneity in the formal political and educational systems at the national level.

The Homogeneity of a Group

If national unity is a product of politics and education in Japan, and if Japan is, in fact, culturally diverse, where is homogeneity? It is most clearly seen in Japanese-style groups that show a strong cohesion and intimacy among insiders against outsiders.

John T. Tadrozny's *Dictionary of Social Science* (1959) provides a concise working definition of *group* in four basic categories as follows:

> group—(1) a number of interacting persons who are aware of being members of a more or less permanent social unit which has some organization and division of functions, something of a status system, some recognized norms to control their conduct, and some similarity of interests or purposes; (2) any number of people who interact even though there may be no organization, division of functions, status system, norms, or sense of permanence among them, a crowd; (3) all the people holding allegiance to certain ideals or purposes, whether they are organized or not, whether they are aware of each other or not, or whether they actually interact directly or not; for example, a labor union, ethnic group, nationality, or nation; (4) human interactions, as such.

In this discussion, the first and third definitions apply. But what must be stressed first of all is the fundamental separation of these two categories. Shared language and knowledge, a result of centralization and standardization of acquired knowledge through education, are mistakenly assumed to be proof of a homogeneity that shapes the Japanese mind. On the contrary, every Japanese is not born with the same degree of "Japaneseness." Innate Japaneseness is a myth, arising from the confusing notion that the homogeneity of a group results from the common nationality of its constituents.

A vast body of literature has been produced about the characteristics of Japanese groups because they are widely thought to be the source of Japanese economic success. Starting with Chie Nakane and continuing to Eshun Hamaguchi, the opinion leaders of the modern culture of technology have emphasized, without exception, that Japanese society is held together by hierarchical group organization, which necessarily enforces on its members a collective orientation and thus represses individualism. The psychological demand for such social organization is believed to be derived from the quality of Japaneseness. It has been rationalized that Japan's emphasis on hierarchical social organization and promotion of the sense of Japanese uniqueness are responsible for the rejection in society of individualistic and less homogeneous alternatives.

The characteristics considered to be unique to Japanese groups are as follows: A Japanese group stands separately from other groups, independent and autonomous, and develops its own culture and identity. In other words, it is localized and closed to others— not only to foreigners but also to other Japanese. Each group develops its own unique qualities whose values are often incomprehensible to outsiders. Through submission to the culture of the group, its members become indispensable and homogeneous parts of the whole. Cohesion in the group is strong enough that members who leave are labelled not only disloyal but defectors.

This homogeneous group orientation has been used to great advantage by large Japanese corporations and the central government. It is based on a lifetime employment system, closed to outsiders. Membership at the lowest level of the hierarchy can be gained after graduation from an institution of higher learning. In principle, then, a person has only one chance in a lifetime to join a group. Yet once membership is secure, that person is assured of employment until retirement. The security factor is built into the Japanese employment system as a nonmonetary benefit, and entrance into such a group carries with it the associative benefit of membership in a highly exclusive and prestigious elite. The social organization insures and takes care of its members for life, and, in exchange, the members are loyal to the organization and identify themselves as homogeneous parts of it. The professional work ethics of corporate groups form the basis for the moral framework of the society.

Recently the lifetime employment system has been revised to take into account the evaluation of the relative merit of workers and has thus introduced greater mobility within the group structure. Yet despite criticism that the resultant mobility is fatal to group loyalties, it has actually served to strengthen the system. Elites have become even more exclusive, because introducing evaluative standards based on merit has given elites the freedom to dismiss colleagues who are less desirable or productive.

Groupism is dependent upon the intimate relationships that it fosters among its members, and solidarity is maintained through psychologically censoring the negative emotional elements that could potentially threaten it. The directors of a leading high-tech company described to me their way of controlling jealousy, easily triggered in relationships within the workplace. When one person is promoted to a managerial position over his colleagues, he does not receive a salary increase until his new superior position is approved by his former colleagues, which takes years. In other words, a newly promoted person has to work harder with much heavier responsibilities, but receives no other compensation besides the prestige attached to his new status. By the time he has received a salary raise, the negative feelings from his hierarchical inferiors are well-settled.

Psychological censoring takes the form of mutual adjustment to a new situation by allowing a necessary passage of time. It indicates that the cohesion of a homogeneous group is the result of controlled social processes, not a spontaneous manifestation of innate Japaneseness.[9]

Structural Pluralism

Ironically, the homogeneity of the group culture has created in Japan a cultural pluralism. Aggressions, carefully controlled and removed from competition among the insiders of a group, are intensely expressed in the competition with other groups and their members. The development of local and independent identity in each isolated group makes communication with other groups more difficult, and therefore more difficult in Japanese society in general. Each group in Japan is a localized (if not ethnic) minority that struggles to advance in relation to other groups. However, in terms of political organization, Japanese tend to join together under a general umbrella of categorization, creating an overlapping definition of their own groups.

The American economist Peter Drucker perceived this competitive dynamic between Japanese groups before the Japanese themselves acknowledged its presence. Drucker's language is often offensive to Japanese, but his insights into Japanese group behavior are surely accurate:

> No group is expected to be completely unselfish or to advocate policies which might cost money, power or votes; Japan's Confucian tradition distrusts self-sacrifice as unnatural.[10] Each group is, however, expected to fit its self-interests into a framework of national needs, national goals, national aspiration, and national values. Sometimes, this expectation produces blatant hypocrisy, as when Japanese physicians demand near-total exemption from taxes as concern for the nation's health. Still, the physicians pay at least lip service to the rule that demands the question, "What is the national interest?" be asked first.[11]

The question here is why the Japanese tend to overlook their own cultural diversity, in contrast to Americans who stress differences among themselves. In trying to answer this question, two points may be made. First, the Japanese have adopted the theories of Japanese homogeneity invented by Americans, in spite of the traditional Japanese claim that Japan is too unique to be understood by anyone but the Japanese. Second, the homogeneity achieved within a group blocks its members from seeing social reality outside the group. Each member is wrapped in layers of his own group sentiment, augmented by the ethos of the group. The Greek word *ethos* has been co-opted by the Japanese language as *etosu*. As a result, the individual member of a group projects his deep emotional conviction in group homogeneity into Japan as a nation. This projection has been crucial to the formation of a sense of Japanese nationalism. At the same time, it has obscured the actual high level of competition and variation that occurs in Japan today.

Individuals as Defective Members of a Group

Eshun Hamaguchi, a socialist, is one of the major theorists who have led the development of Japan's modern culture of technology. In asserting that groupism is the most essential value in the contemporary culture, Hamaguchi discredits the role of individualism in the culture:

Harmony in the work situation is a secondary matter for Westerners who believe in individualism. They think it is enough if each member fulfills his own responsibilities. However, in Japanese organizations, the task group constitutes the unit of responsibility and when any problem arises the members of the division or the department cover it. Without harmony there is no organization. . . . However, Japanese administrators who believe absolutely in the principles of modern bureaucracy that originated in the West tend to be suspicious of "harmony among people." And the younger generations who have been educated since the end of the War and who want individualistic independence feel it painful to be forced to integrate themselves into the group under the spirit of "harmony" and will show resistance. The harmonious tendency which is part of the inborn nature of the Japanese is not always treated positively today. However, the "multiple effect" of harmony is not negligible. The output of work done by a well-harmonized group rather than individuals is far larger than the simple sum of the individuals' work. The outstanding efficiency of Japanese firms is the result of such harmony, and the modernization of Japan, in fact, depends on this group orientation.[12]

Hamaguchi further clarifies and defines the differences:

An "individual," as a modern personality typically observed in the West, holds a conviction that he is a firmly established substance which is solely independent, and, therefore, cannot be invalidated by others. Also, he is convinced that he is the master of himself, but at the same time that he is liable for his own deeds. The individual objectifies such an assertion (that he is undoubtedly himself) and the sense of autonomy. The consciousness of self which appears in this process has been conceptualized as "ego." Key concepts in psychology and psychoanalysis including *self* and *ego* have been constructed under such a model of human being. Ericson's "ego-identity" may be understood as a social application of it.[13]

In contrast to this Western concept of individualism, Hamaguchi presents a Japanese model of man as follows:

for the Japanese, "self" means the portion which is distributed to him, according to the situation he is in, from the living space shared between himself and the other person with whom he had developed a mutually dependent relationship.

A reason why this self-consciousness of the Japanese is formed this way is probably that self and others are in a symbiotic relationship, and that they believe that their beings depend largely on others' beings. Makoto Hoshino writes that it is common (for the Japanese) that they first have the feeling of oneness with others, and that this feeling ensures the being of self. This relativistic "self" can be easily mistaken for being unindependent . . . and also primitive in personality development. However, here, selves are "mutually dependent," and their spontaneous fulfillment of the needs are intentionally controlled. Self-control to relate to others is a fully mature behavioral pattern.[14]

Hamaguchi calls such mutually dependent persons "contextual men," because in relationships with others, they are guided by values determined in the social context. The values that are upheld are oneness with, and compassion for, others. Exhibiting compassion is as central to Japanese moral life as is the moral concept of love in Christian societies. Through shared feelings, contextual men share their fate. The feeling of mutual fate becomes particularly strong when it is expressed within economic groups, such as business corporations. The members of corporations develop unlimited sympathy toward each other, immediately respond to others with expressions of deep and serious concern, and appreciate others' expressions of happiness or grief in response to their needs. Group members interpret these sympathetic responses as proof of the authenticity of the group's homogeneity and ethos. Intimate friendship, a strong theme in Japanese literature and art, is so emotionally profound for the Japanese that it is difficult for them not to hold a prejudice against individualistic societies that they must be lacking in this essential component of humanity, since the Japanese cannot conceive of it developing except collectively.

Yet the proponents of groupism tend to ignore what their own arguments indicate, that oneness and compassion do not extend beyond the members of a group. Such moral values are not universal but limited in scope. Talcott Parsons first presented this point using the term *particularism,* which was later applied to Japanese society by Robert Bellah.[15]

As much as there is a "fully mature behavioral pattern" among insiders to reassure their bonding with each other, there is at work an equally mature pattern of avoidance between an insider and an outsider. The same behavior carries different social meaning, depending on whom one is interacting with. An action that binds insiders together will not necessarily bind an insider to an outsider. For example, compassion may be directed toward an outsider, but the meaning of the gesture changes from an expression of oneness to an expression of charity. Charity is defined here as a nonbinding expression of goodwill that does not create or reinforce mutual intimacy.

This dependency on social context for the meaning of social behavior is what led Parsons to invoke his concept of particularism. Hamaguchi's contextual men have totally submitted themselves to the orientation of a group and internalized the particularistic codes of the group in their personal morality. As group members, Japanese are expected to vary their attitude according to the contextual definition of a social situation. This is why Japanese may appear to display contradictory characteristics. Ruth Benedict (1946) noted that when one thing is said about the Japanese, the opposite is always true about them.[16] This reflexive social behavior is an integral part of the Japanese ethos; yet it may not be unique to Japanese culture, as has been frequently assumed, but an inevitable result of such a social orientation itself. It is important to make the distinction that this alternation of attitude is a moral action rather than a moral compromise.

Groupism as an Historical Value

Social scientists have generally agreed that the farming household of traditional Japan is the basis for the model of groupism. Examining the model clarifies how the ideological basis of groupism was founded and how individualism is more than simply deviant in the culture. Such farming households were still fairly common, especially in the northern part of Japan, until World War II.[17] According to the traditional native definition, the members of a given clan claim to be the descendants of the same male ancestor identified through the paternal line. However, through more recent research, it has become evident that the membership of a household also contained non-blood "kin," who technically should have been excluded from clan membership. In addition to blood ties, membership by adoption, marriage, and for economic reasons was allowed. When a household did not have a male successor, it was common practice to adopt one by creating a quasi-biological relationship. Married women identified themselves through the fathers of their husbands, rather than through their biological fathers. Those who joined the group for economic reasons were usually servants and tenants of the household, who identified their masters and landlords as quasi-fathers. Yet there was a clear distinction between "true" kin, those who were integrated into the household through adoption or marriage, and "fictive" kin, those who joined the household through an economic relationship.

Thus the Japanese group has traditionally expanded the definition of kinship from a strictly biological one to one more widely inclusive, through cultural manipulation; in this way it develops networks of human relationships in the work situation based on superior-inferior status differences, analogous to the parent-child relationship. In this social context, Confucianism was adopted from China among the *samurai*, the ruling class in Japan; the fundamental ethic of filial piety was more actively applied to the relationship between a lord and his subjects than the real biological relationship between parents and children. A lord and his subjects entered a quasi-parent-child relationship, which was socially given a higher priority over the biological one, unlike the Confucianism practiced in China.

This is one reason why the Japanese consider their companies as family, not as the communal types of social organizations Americans perceive them to be. Thus, Akio Morita, chairman of Sony, claims that the family-like orientation of company management is the key to success:

> There is no secret ingredient or hidden formula responsible for the success of the best Japanese companies. No theory or plan or government policy will make a business a success; that can only be done by people. The most important mission for a Japanese manager is to develop a healthy relationship with his employees, to create a family-like feeling within the corporation, a feeling that employees and managers share the same fate. Those companies that are most successful in Japan are those that have managed to create a shared sense of fate among all employees, what Americans call labor and management, and the shareholders.[18]

As families do, Japanese companies function as self-contained welfare systems. The members are bound by the quasi-parent-child relationships to which they have submitted. In giving up a sense of freedom, members gain great economic and psychological security. This security, however, cannot be provided unless the company itself is economically secure. Security is a property of the establishment and, accordingly, is an ostensible quality of the elite's culture.

The same cultural version of a biological relationship functions also to give the modern Japanese a strong sense of Japaneseness, although, as I have pointed out earlier, this cultivated sense has been misidentified as having "innate" origins. In fact, both biological and social factors serve to qualify one for membership in any group, although it is perceived to be innate. Those who believe in the uniqueness of the Japanese commonly hold that to be a "fully qualified" Japanese, one must be born in Japan from Japanese parents, one must grow up in Japan, and one should not stay abroad longer than five years. Membership in a group is primarily biological, but it can be easily mitigated by non-biological conditions. Japaneseness is vulnerable. This means that biological qualities must be and can only be maintained and preserved through careful control of the environment.

This cultural interpretation of biological relations is fundamental to Japanese naturalism, a traditional aspect of contemporary Japanese culture. For example, a woman is a woman by birth, but to maintain that given quality, she must carefully protect her femininity. She is expected to be *"onna rashii,"* literally "to be feminine," but implying "to become closer to the real nature of Woman." The underlying message is that preserving her given nature is enabled by removing social and human conditions that block her from the oneness with her own nature. Similarly, men are expected to be masculine, and workers are also expected to become closer to the real working nature of human being.

Ruth Benedict saw this clearly but seemingly with some surprise:

> Human nature in Japan, they say, is naturally good and to be trusted. It does not need to fight an evil half of itself. It needs to cleanse the window of its soul and act with appropriateness on every different occasion. It has allowed itself to become "dirt": impurities are readily removed and man's essential goodness shines forth again. Buddhist philosophy has gone farther in Japan than in any other nation in teaching that every man is a potential Buddha and that rules of virtue are not in the sacred writing but in what one uncovers within one's own enlightened and innocent soul. Why should one distrust what one finds there? No evil is inherent in man's soul. They have no theology which cries with the Psalmist, "Behold, I was shapen in iniquity, and in sin did my mother conceive me." They teach no doctrine of the Fall of Man. "Human feelings" are blessings which a man should not condemn. Neither the philosopher nor the peasant does condemn them.[19]

According to naturalism, it is usually assumed that the given nature is good and that a human being can be good as long as he maintains oneness with his nature. He can, however, easily be blocked from his nature in the process of becoming an adult, when such human and social conditions as aspirations for wealth and prestige are assimilated. In the traditional belief system, a person is born innocent and becomes defiled as he becomes separated from his own good nature. But he can recover his oneness through controlling the self and the social environment with wisdom. Hence, education is given an essential role, because knowledge is considered to be a major component of wisdom. The logic of the achievement of oneness with good nature is neatly captured in a saying from the Japanese art of flower arranging: "Be more natural than nature itself."

The Japanese belief system which provided such rationales for living was disdained after World War II and has not been incorporated into today's secular social system. This is why the myth of Japanese oneness that supports groupism is confusing. The belief is commonly held, but its rationale is unclear, even to the holder of the belief. Although some individuals in art and religion have been articulate about the belief system, they are considered socially marginal, as are certain revivalists in religious movements, who are trying actively to reinstate the traditional belief system and are thought of as religiously heterodox.

Inevitable Fear of Individualism

It is clear why there is a deep fear of individualism among those who have built the modern culture of technology in Japan. The ideology of naturalism, which covertly insures groupism as the natural state of the Japanese, is under constant threat from surrounding social conditions, of which individualism is a large part. To those who identify Japanese tradition with groupism, individualism appears as a total import from the West or as a mutation due to changes in the social environment under the pressures of Westernization.

Those who claim to be or are labelled individualistic are considered to be not only nonconformist but also antitraditional, anti-Japanese, and antisocial. If groupism is good, then by definition individualism is bad. If the former has brought prosperity to Japan, then the latter will destroy it. If group identity provides security through large and established social organizations, then individualism provides only insecurity and disunity that will lead to unrest. As has been noted, in the Japanese social context, security is not only physical and economic but psychological and moral as well. A member of a powerful and established organization gains a share of the prestige of his company by identifying himself as an indispensable part of the whole. Prestige provides a degree of power over others through its command of respect and honor. Individuals on the periphery, having no powerful organization to identify with, cannot achieve the same level of prestige. Although such an individual may become rich, his wealth does not bring him automatic prestige. Money can buy many things, but not respect from others. In order for the wealthy outside of the economic mainstream to gain respect, they must in effect enter the mainstream by constructing their own corporations built on groupist structures. This closed cycle between the mainstream and the periphery has kept the Japanese basically conservative and their society basically secure.

In this traditional cycle in the modern Japanese economy, entrepreneurs on the periphery willingly give up their peripheral status in order to gain status in the mainstream. Without status, they as individuals are kept in a position inferior to the established mainstream social organization. This cycle is not dialectical. According to the principles of groupism, Japanese social organizations remain exclusive by isolating each other. The interaction between different social organizations occurs through a process of limited access, and members are prohibited from full association with outsiders. Closedness and self-containment in a social organization are synonymous with prestige. The coexistence of self-contained social organizations and cultural pluralism does designate social options but dynamic interaction is not possible.

In contrast to this traditional cycle in the modern Japanese economy, some entrepreneurial individuals on the periphery have taken the stance of choosing to remain there, taking advantage of the existing structural pluralism. By choosing to remain on the periphery, they have put themselves in a position of antithesis to the economic mainstream. This is a new social phenomenon, and is, to a certain extent, Hegelian. It will create momentum to generate domestic dynamic social interaction, without external intervention in Japanese society. The first champions of this movement were those who led the fashion industry in the 1970s, and now, the members of the high-tech industry are its rising stars. Their common denominator is creativity, which thrives more often in independent minds than in those dependent on collectivity. Further, individualism and independence have high potential both domestically and externally; they are creating openness to foreign businesses, providing an advantage to foreign trade in addition to domestic growth. The position of individualistic entrepreneurs is much stronger today than it appears on the surface of Japanese society.

Notes

1. The first attempts to create a synthesis between traditional Japanese values and Western values were embodied and consistently employed in the motto, "Japanese spirit, Western technology." However, the Japanese defeat in 1945 was thought to testify that the attempted synthesis had failed; the motto was banned as part of the postwar ideology, and more recent attempts to form a synthesis have been comparatively clandestine and less declamatory.
2. Kim, 1988.
3. Watanabe, 1985.
4. Yamamoto, 1983, p. 35.
5. Ibid., p. 210.
6. Ibid., p. 143.
7. Ibid., p. 203.
8. Today, it is understood in America that the Japanese are particular and demanding about their consumption. American business consultants now agree that by trying to please users who are difficult to please, the quality of production improves, and, as a result, sales increase.
9. The characteristics of the Japanese group have been widely discussed since Chie Nakane's contributions. It may be noted here that a larger group may contain smaller subgroups. And a person may function as a member of the larger and smaller groups at the same time, in such a way that he is both a Japanese and a member of a local group, or that he is a Mitsubishi man and the member of a division of Mitsubishi, which is usually in competition with other divisions. Here, he is competitive with other Mitsubishi men outside his division, but he is expected to harmonize with Mitsubishi as a whole.
10. This view of Confucianism may be puzzling to Asians.
11. Drucker, 1988, p. 205.
12. Hamaguchi, 1983, pp. 125–6.
13. Ibid., pp. 140–1.
14. Ibid., p. 142.

15. Robert Bellah's argument putting forth the concept of particularism in Japan is still considered controversial among the Japanese.
16. Ruth Benedict's remarks on the Japanese contradictory personality have been quoted by many Japanologists and journalists.
17. The family organization in a rural setting was first systematically explored by Kozaemon Ariga and Takao Tsuchiya in 1935–6. Their report, which was published in several volumes, was summarized by Michio Nagai in English in 1953. Later, the family was further conceptualized into the household by Chie Nakane (1967), and the stem family was identified by Harumi Befu in 1971. Some Japanese sociologists claim that the Japanese family is too uniquely Japanese to be rendered into any other language equivalent, and refer to it only as the Japanese *ie*.
18. Morita, 1986, p. 130.
19. Benedict, 1969, pp. 191–2.

2

Growing Individualism on the Periphery

Individualism in Entrepreneurship

The structural pluralism of Japanese society has permitted individualists to pursue independent lifestyles in the cultural vacuum at the periphery. Their existence has been overlooked in the nationwide preoccupation with upward mobility, with gaining access to the privileged economic mainstream through academic achievement. With the emergence of the New Men, whose same goals had been pursued by a number of individualists in the older generation for some time, young people holding individualistic values came to public attention, causing a degree of consternation.

One researcher, whom I will call Kazuo Kawashima, told me, "I like to work for a cause. But I do not want my boss to tell me to do this or do that. Even in an organization, as long as we make the effort to insist on our own needs, we can bend the established order. I have known quite a few people who do this."

Kawashima, in his late thirties, suggests that he is far from alone in his unorthodox work style and attitudes. Clearly, the New Men are not really new. While stating his obedience to the rules, Kawashima at the same time wishes to "bend" the establishment. This attitude is a defining feature of New Men individualism.

Kawashima also has unorthodox family attitudes. To begin with, his wife is Mexican. He says, "My wife is a good partner when I go to developing countries. Since I married her, my world has expanded. She is very different from me, and makes me aware of

how Japanese I am." He also says, "I am not interested in achieving higher positions. Since my wife is pregnant now, fifty to seventy
percent of my attention goes to her."

According to an investor I interviewed, the most difficult type of
New Men or individuals to manage are those who are qualified for
but not interested in promotion. Kawashima fits into this category.
The investor says, "Those interested in promotion are the easiest
to manage. They work hard, without given instructions, hoping to
display their ability. Those who are unable and apathetic are not so
difficult to manage either. They will follow the given instructions
under the given framework. It is our task to set up a good framework for them. They are too weak to stand up and complain. They
are harmless."

Another businessman, a fifty-year-old owner of a business news
company, whom I will call Akimori Shibata, also gave me an
interesting response. He, unlike other Japanese men of his generation, declares that he would choose his wife over his work. He
says, "We are both independent. We decide independently if we
should work or what kind of work we should take. We divide our
household tasks equally, including the child care." Although it is
traditionally the case that men refrain from any household tasks,
Shibita explained himself, saying, "I grew up in a farming family in
Shizuoka Prefecture [where farmers are traditionally wealthy], and
in my home it was a rule that anyone who was available did the
household tasks. The male-female distinction did not matter. My
father worked in the kitchen when my mother was busy in the field.
No one felt ashamed to cook or clean up the house. The real
Japanese tradition is not at all like the kind which has been posited
in theories." Shibata was referring to the ideas promoted by the
opinion leaders of the modern culture of technology.

His case certainly illustrates the diversity of Japanese culture.[1]
Yet Shibata's experience has not been translated into a cultural
trend and survives only marginally. Shibata continued, "I enjoy
doing household tasks. The work unrelated to money-making is
relaxing. While my wife cooks, I clean up the house. We take turns
taking care of our children. When we are both busy, we hire
someone. Japanese men are not independent people. They work in

their companies and do nothing else. Because they have no way to discharge their frustration, they become workaholics.''

A declaration of self- and family-orientation is close to a denial of the prevailing cultural authority. Kiyoto Otani (another pseudonym), in responding to my inquiries, explained his radical view of the Emperor as no more than a symbol of groupism and the denial of individual ability. He explained that because the succession to the throne was determined by birth, it is a contradiction of the basic principles of meritocracy, achievement through competition on an individual level. He says that having the Emperor as a national symbol makes him feel physically uncomfortable. Yet he is not interested in politics. He is a businessman, and his interests are concentrated in making money and on his family.

The combination of such radicalism and conservatism has puzzled some in the status quo, because they expect that radical individualism belongs with politically deviant minority groups. In the 1960s, Otani's kind of individualism was expressed more collectively by political youth movements. Twenty years ago, the youth wanted to change the political framework through protest. Today, they are looking for more freedom within the framework. This is the main reason why those of the older generations criticize the young for being "conservative" in spite of their "individualist" attitudes. From the elders' point of view, Otani, who resists authority but is indifferent to the replacement of the existing political framework, fits the definition of the New Men.

Tetsuo Iwasaki, president of Applied Materials Japan (AMJ), an American-owned high-tech company in Japan, says, "Professors tried to make me their student," meaning that he has pursued his studies without relying on the guidance of authority. It is true that universities are the most conservative sector of Japanese society, standing at the top of the culture and providing access to the mainstream. Unlike the American system, education in Japan is the foundation of the nation, and professors are recognized and respected as top authorities. Overcoming the fear of authority is difficult, and the central position that academics hold in the path to the mainstream makes it extremely hard to circumvent the system.

The numerous Japanese whom I met with who considered themselves individualists did not consider themselves to be either exceptional or deviant. They commonly responded that they had many friends who shared their views.

Ichikazu Yanagida, owner of a small high-tech company, had to choose to go to a technical school instead of a university, because his father failed in his own business while Yanagida was in high school. His experimental style in business has brought him widespread recognition, and he was recently invited as a special guest to a prestigious international conference in France. Due in part to the success of his business and in part to the choices he made while young, he does not hold the group orientation so cherished by the modern culture of technology in high regard.

Yukiko Hanai, whom I have mentioned earlier, agreed with Yanagida. When I asked her why she decided to participate in the new working hours and privileged working conditions granted to women specialists such as designers and patterners, changes that go against the common work ethic, she replied that she had never worried about what others were thinking or doing. Her decision not to attend university was made with the same resolution.

Tetsuo Iwasaki took only night classes during his university days; he wanted to learn about business without wasting time, as he felt day students did. Although he majored in the humanities, he mastered the basic knowledge of high-tech products that the trading company he worked for dealt in, so that he could get into sales. He had no prior knowledge, and he photocopied materials at work and studied them by himself at home. He recalls, laughingly, "The bookkeeping division of my company asked my section leader why the xerox expenses of my section were extremely high, but, of course, he did not know." Later, when he was recruited by an American company, he taught himself English. He said, "Attending business meetings was the best practice for English, although at the beginning, I could hardly understand what they were talking about." In the regular part of entrance examinations, Japanese students are taught English grammar and some useful expressions. But, in Iwasaki's case, English was learned as part of an interaction with native speakers. In doing so, he assimilated the language and the culture together. He was observant enough to see language as a social process among individuals. Japanese education does not in general prepare for this kind of associative communication.

It is interesting that Iwasaki's individuality has been better appreciated by an American than a Japanese company, although his personal identity is thoroughly Japanese. Yet he has become Americanized to the extent that when a conflict arises, he can be confrontational, even with his Japanese colleagues, rather than responding in the traditional way of either avoiding the conflict or seeking to alleviate it by harmonious means.

Individualists in Every Age Group

Here, it is important to clarify why individualists, those older than the New Men individualists, appear to be confined to the age group between thirty-five and fifty years. The fact is that they are simply the first postwar generation to become visible. In a society where seniority is more respected than youth, many youths preparing for future careers are not often in public view. And older individualists also attest that they spent their twenties learning the expertise to express their talents. Even Kansai Yamamoto, who openly claims that he did not pay much attention to the business side of fashion in the beginning, spent several years intensively learning design and technique. During this period, he kept a low profile in the fashion industry.

Today, individualists in the younger generation are more conservative than their predecessors. Yet the silence among younger individuals involved in entrepreneurial experiments should not be taken as an indication of their nonexistence. They are aware that they are working on potential, which is fragile until they can build up confidence and achievement. Even those who have already been recognized for their talent hesitate to speak decisively. Prior to gaining economic independence, they are usually necessarily employed by companies that can offer them a chance to develop skills. Their future success depends on their ability, during this period, to cultivate the psychological strength to stand outside of groupism. By the age of thirty, they begin to become independent and often have gained good reputations for their talent and skills. Moreover, they have assimilated the knowledge of relationships indispensable in handling marketing and production in Japanese culture. If they are developing great self-confidence, they also become more comfortable about articulating their own histories. They are looking forward to a time when they, too, will have success stories to relate.

Incubator for Individualists

Individualistic entrepreneurs tend to value the particular talents of their employees more highly and specifically than do larger and more established companies in the mainstream. Entrepreneurial companies are more dependent on individual abilities and performance than team work, which is a major feature of groupism. For example, in the fashion industry, owners and workers have a great deal of respect for the nonrational, emotional, and nonbusinesslike aspects of life, such as expressions of passion and sentiment. A result is that management in this industry shows a high degree of flexibility. According to my own survey among managers of active smaller businesses in the fashion industry, respondents said that they gladly pay better wages to workers who show greater ability and try to create the best working conditions for them.

One entrepreneurial owner of her own company did emphasize that she encourages her employees to have close and long-lasting business relationships with their clients, an essential in the traditional Japanese growth economy. She also values long-standing relationships between herself and her employees. She discourages her employees' attempts to expand by becoming independent, since she feels they will do well because they are under her protection. However, she added that if employees insisted on leaving, she would not do anything to prevent them. Although many entrepreneurial business owners share this attitude, and while some even encourage employee independence, most owners must rely on their workers' sense of loyalty, as they cannot encourage them to remain with wage incentives that they cannot provide. Yet, like group-structured mainstream businesses, these owners rarely dismiss an employee, echoing a sense of security akin to that found in larger companies. In the best entrepreneurial companies, security and mobility exist in balance. Many individualists begin their careers this way, gaining knowledge, skills, and social credit in a small company, and leaving the company during their thirties. The smaller businesses function as an incubator for individualists, in the same way that the entrepreneurs who employ them became self-made achievers.

Work Enthusiasm Among Individualists

The enthusiasm among individualists and self-made business owners is another notable contribution they have made to the economy. The mainstream holds the misconception that individualism is synonymous with social apathy, but entrepreneurial individualists love to work. In fact, a few of them took issue with my question, "How would you evaluate the work ethic?" They thought I was motivated to ask because I was critical of the work ethic in Japan and that I was implying that it was a bad social custom.

Akiko Arai, owner of her own textile design firm with five full-time employees, told me: "I forced myself to work hard when I was younger. It was necessary to do so, until I had mastered all of the basic techniques to design fabrics. I used to consider working hard a poor choice of lifestyle. But now I feel happy working hard for myself and being creative."

Yukiko Hanai, a leading fashion designer, said, "Working is a creative job that suits me wonderfully. I try to excavate buried feelings and refresh them. I am always trying to find something unknown of the dignity in the soul of human beings. This is my personality. And I am always thinking of it in my daily life. The results are evident in my work." Of her workers, to whom she gives privileged working conditions, she added, "Most in my company are specialists whose products can be infinitely joyful, depending on their own creativity." Like other independent and creative people, Arai has little time off. "But," she says, "I like leisure time, too. Every year, I manage to give myself ten days off and take a trip abroad. Such trips are inspiring."

Kiyoto Otani's (pseudonym) comments sum up the work ethic as it is interpreted by Japan's contemporary individualists:

I fully support the traditional work ethic. Those who refuse to work should not eat. To live a lazy life, one has to cheat. Hard-working people should be rewarded. Too many able and excellent human beings have been taken advantage of. . . . There are two kinds of genius. One is found in spending money to create new values, and the other is found in allocating the resources and funding to provide the first, by cheating the idiots who cannot imagine change in the status quo. But to enable this social process, social mobility must be ensured. In Japan, the educational system blocks it. However, business provides the momentum needed for such a process.

Meritocratic Reformation

In the late 1980s, it was widely believed that the kind of social mobility which entrepreneurial individualists wanted was within reach. There appeared an increasing exchange of workers between the mainstream and the periphery of the Japanese economy. Some individualists entered large and established corporations; their acceptance at the junior executive level had a strong impact on the seniority system. Many Japanese concluded that this was the end of the lifetime employment system of the establishment upon which socio-economic security depended.

In the traditional system, with its lifetime employment and seniority aspects, promotion is possible only from within the company. A company man would compete only with his colleagues of the same age group for a position one level higher than his own. Unlike the American system, there was a structural hindrance to the possibility of going into a company position in another firm. An employee could advance only from within the company, and newcomers were relegated to the most inferior positions. Therefore, the exchange of workers newly starting between firms appeared to reflect a restructuring in the modern culture of technology. The reality is, however, that if one looks more closely these revisions have served to rationalize and strengthen the existing system. Large and established companies still are basically closed.

The Japanese government published a report[2] showing that the rate of occupational changes in 1987 were much higher than in 1982, in all age groups, for both men and women. Men in the twenty-five to thirty-four year-old group showed a 50 percent increase in job shifts; the increase for forty-five to fifty-four year-olds was 80 percent; and 60 percent for those between sixty and sixty-four years-old. Among women, there was a seventy percent increase in the twenty-five to thirty-four year-old group, and a one hundred percent rise for women between the ages of forty-five and forty-nine. While the report indicates increasing mobility in Japanese society, it does not answer questions about the degree of upward mobility.

High mobility among older age groups does not indicate a step-up in employment. Larger companies have lately adopted a peculiarly Japanese form of meritocracy, where older and less productive employees are encouraged to leave and "helped" through company career planning centers to relocate. Until recently, this group of employees was the most protected and privileged under the lifetime employment system, and they received the highest range of salaries. Discharging them is a great benefit for the company that wants to cut personnel costs by replacing them with a younger and cheaper work force.

Trading companies were the first to institute this change. C. Ito established its new division called the Career Planning Center in 1981. Between 1981 and 1987, the center assisted 320 persons to change their occupations. Their average age was fifty-two, and one third were C. Ito employees. From dealing only with its own employees, the C. Ito center soon expanded to deal with people from other companies. The president of the Career Center says, "Step-up for older people is difficult. Except for those who have a truly excellent and special ability, one's income will be reduced by 20 to 25 percent."[3]

Companies providing for career change numbered only twenty-four in 1975, but swelled to eighty-three by 1987.[4] The president of Tokyo Executive Search says, "In the past, eight out of ten used to hang up on me when I stated the purpose of my call. An employee contacting us himself used to indicate a betrayal of his company and his colleagues, who were making self-sacrifices in order to form a team necessary for maintaining the lifetime employment. But now, eight out of ten respond as if they had been waiting for my call."[5]

By discharging older workers, even elite companies, which used to be completely closed to all but recent college graduates, are opening positions to those who are young, but already trained in their fields. The highest demand is for those with training in high-tech science, engineering, and financing. Although this appears on the surface to indicate a relaxing of the Japanese social structure, the following conditions, which apply to existing employment mobility, show the limitations of the changes: First, change becomes more difficult in direct relation to increasing age. One's income level may increase by moving to new positions until one reaches the mid-thirties, but will decrease if any change is made after that. Thus, although older age groups form the major categories of the job-shift population, their mobility usually is downward. Second, having more than one skill, such as managerial ability and mastery of a foreign language, or a science background and management experience, increases one's chances for a better position. Fulfilling these conditions is unusual in older age groups. Third, in a new job, the benefits of lifetime security may not be provided, indicating that a new job is often found on the periphery and that the shift is downward. Fourth, if the shift occurs from a large company to a smaller one, the smaller company will invariably be characterized by a lesser degree of teamwork approach, indicating more difficulties for older workers formerly trained and accustomed to team work. In the smaller company, an individual worker's abilities may thus be more rigorously tested than in a larger company. And finally, the new employer is looking for a worker who can actively and quickly adjust to a number of responsibilities, without having a period of growing into responsibilities that is built into the lifetime employment system.[6]

Hence, in a wider perspective, there are two major flows of workers: first, the older workers moving downward from the mainstream to the periphery; second, the young and well-trained workers from either the periphery to the mainstream, or from within the mainstream to another position there. In other words, established companies draw able workers who have already been employed, in addition to the traditional recruitment from recent university graduates. A polarization between younger and older workers has emerged. The opening of the mainstream to an additional category of individuals has brought with it the exclusion of a second category, that of older workers. The result of the opening of the mainstream, instead of creating free flows between itself and the periphery, has further strengthened it.

Those employers on the periphery are frustrated by the situation.

Tetsuo Iwasaki, a self-made entrepreneur, has no sympathy for older workers who have been pressured to leave the lifetime employment system. When he offered two-year contracts to several such workers, he found that they all wanted a minimum contract of five years. Iwasaki said, "Even after they were discharged by the establishment, and were made to realize that lifetime employment was no longer theirs to demand, they still asked for the same security in my company."

Although discharging older workers is common in the mainstream today, companies are still embarrassed to have those at the executive and managerial levels leave, and "dropping out" from an executive position at an established company is rare. In response to my queries about individuals who had left their companies for independent pursuits, directors in a well-known high-tech manufacturing firm avoided directly answering and tried hard to give me the impression that there were few such occurrences. The following is an extract from my interviews:

QUESTION: Are there any people who wished to become independent and did actually leave your company?

DIRECTOR A: No, there is no such person . . . maybe one several years ago.

DIRECTOR B: Ah . . . yes, one person left.

QUESTION: Would you know what he is doing now?

DIRECTOR B: Not really. But he was a good person.

DIRECTOR A: I wonder what he is now.

QUESTION: Could you think of any more like him?

DIRECTOR A: Umm . . . maybe one other person. But I am not sure.

DIRECTOR B: . . . I am not sure.

In the lifetime employment and seniority system, older employees who are well paid do not necessarily occupy executive positions. An older employee who does the same work as a younger one nevertheless receives a much higher salary. Discharging these kinds of older workers is a great economic advantage to the company, but losing executives is not. It is considered shameful for the company when this does happen, since the company feels that such disloyalty will be interpreted as meaning that the "culture" of its atmosphere is somehow inadequate.

Mobility Within the Periphery

Statistical evidence indicates that there is higher and freer social mobility on the periphery, and there is a correlation between career mobility and the size of the workplace. In a larger business, workers spend an average of 13.1 years in the company before reaching the average wage at the average age of 36.4. This indicates that the average hiring age is twenty-three, the age at which most individuals graduate from four-year universities. In a smaller business, however, the worker spends only 11.4 years before attaining the average wage. But the worker in this case is 39.4 years old, three years older than the average in larger businesses.[7] The statistics suggest there is more mobility and insecurity in the smaller business environment, as well as lower average wages. As long as workers stay in the mainstream, they can expect more prestigious positions than on the periphery. The higher mobility among non-elite enterprises does not imply more opportunity for advancement. Thus, compared to the slow and steady road to success in the mainstream, the patterns of individual success on the periphery vary greatly.

Tetsuo Iwasaki, whom I quoted earlier, represents the higher end of entrepreneurial achievement, and shows a pattern of success not possible in the mainstream. He began his career as a farmer. He had studied journalism as an undergraduate at Nippon University and worked in a print shop. His father's death forced him to leave school in order to tend the family farm. Soon, however, he started work in the sales division of a science materials company. He began to design machines in response to customers' needs, and his resourcefulness earned him the position of section chief at the age of twenty-three, when most people are just entering the job market.

Iwasaki's company made products similar to those of Kanematsu Corporation, and he was assigned to handle disputes with them. When he was seventy-five, Kanematsu itself recruited him to start a new company, Kanematsu Semiconductor. What is unusual about Iwasaki's experience is that although Kanematsu recognized that his ambitions were not limited by his identification with his first employer, Kanematsu itself trusted his sense of loyalty to the extent of offering him a new position. Iwasaki moved forward by cultivating a sense of himself separate from the parent company, while at the same time he was mindful of cultivating the Japanese tradition of actively expanding friendship networks, the primary access to open relationships in Japanese society. (This phenomenon is explored in chapter 3.) He began to feel that he could make his dream come true—a business of his own, run in his style of management.

Because Kanematsu Semiconductor was fully controlled by the Kanematsu Trading Company for its first year, Iwasaki, by default, became a Kanematsu man. He had moved from a small to a much larger company, where English was the lingua franca, the telex was as commonplace as the telephone, and every aspect of the operation appeared well-organized. He became a director at the age of twenty-nine and held his title until he left the company at thirty-two, when he was recruited by one of his major customers, Applied Material (AMT), an American high-tech company employing 1,400 workers. Today, Iwasaki is a vice-president of AMT and president of Applied Materials in Japan, the major branch of AMT where it does 30 percent of its global business. He observed to me that trading companies such as Kanematsu emphasize the importance of knowledge as a precious commodity, but that they are slow in moving to obtain the state-of-the-art expertise demanded by rapidly changing high-tech industry.

Iwasaki displays significant individualist characteristics. He is not ashamed of standing alone, and he is not psychologically occupied with a sense of corporate loyalty; yet at the same time, his energies are focussed on the company. To the upholders of the modern technological culture, he represents a paradox. Akinoir Shibata (pseudonym), who introduced me to Iwasaki, says that he is an unusual man. Iwasaki himself says that he wishes to relate to Americans as an individual who happens to be working in an American company. In doing so, he believes that he is initiating the next step for Japanese business. He wants to be an exemplar for other Japanese in the process of economic internationalization, but he does not want to become a spokesperson, nor does he have any desire to seek political power.

From Entrepreneur to Mainstream: Traditional Pattern

Beyond the success occurring among entrepreneurs remaining on the periphery, there is also a discernable pattern whereby successful entrepreneurs enter the mainstream. In transition, their businesses show a mixture of characteristics from both the mainstream and the periphery. The manager of Bigi, a still-growing firm in the fashion industry, told me that the workers he recently employed are college graduates with no direct business experience. The fact that he has taken on workers with little experience follows the model of the mainstream lifetime employment system. Once hired, however, the employees, except for sales clerks, are subject to some very non-traditional standards. They are evaluated carefully and personally, if not objectively. Bigi's manager maintains that there are no accurately objective standards for measuring artistic potential. But he emphasizes that although quality can be understood only intuitively, it is evident in a worker's creations. He also claims that discrimination against women is nonexistent in his company, a policy not yet taken up by the establishment, despite the government's recent anti-discrimination campaign. Bigi's manager says that more than 50 percent of their employees are women, and that discriminating against women would be bad business policy.

It remains that prestige and security still cannot be captured merely by capturing the capital floating at the periphery of the economy. The mainstream holds these two valuables, and the dream of rich entrepreneurs is yet to join the mainstream and gain prestige by expanding their businesses, then to solidify their status through marriage alliances with the established elite or through sending their sons to top universities. Because Japanese society values security above all, the rich must prove that they will last and that they themselves have become providers, offering lifetime employment to others and by consistently identifying themselves with the production of high-quality merchandise.

With the entrance of peripheral entrepreneurs into the mainstream, the cycle is closed; power originally concentrated in the mainstream absorbs the economic power stored in the periphery, as it accumulates. This cycle will be self-perpetuating, as long as the desire among entrepreneurs to join the mainstream remains strong. Typical of this closed cycle of growth, Sony, Honda, Toyota, Hitachi, and NEC (Nippon Electric Company) developed during the chaos after World War II. A contemporary example is the Yamakuni Company, which began as a subcontractor specializing in welding. In 1970, the company produced the first Japanese aluminum swimming pool in a technological exchange partnership with a West German company. Today, the Yamakuni Company holds 50 percent of the shares in the aluminum and stainless steel swimming pools in the Japanese domestic market. The company has also extended its business from pools to various related equipment and to aluminum bicycles. It is developing a "sports world" in a major resort area under the company motto of "Yamakuni of Sports and Health," in conjunction with ten major companies, including Suntory and Mitsuno, with a total investment of 4.5 billion yen.[8]

Typical Cases

Yoshihiko Otsuka observed two cases of large-scale expansion in the fashion industry. In 1974, Takaya Iwasaki started Person's Inc. with twelve people and one million yen (approximately 7,700 U.S. dollars at the exchange rate of one dollar per 130 yen). The total sales per year reached 300 million yen by 1980, 450 million yen in 1981, 600 million yen in 1982, 1.6 billion yen in 1983, 4 billion yen in 1984, 7 billion yen in 1985, 8 billion yen in 1986, and now approaches 10 billion yen per year. Person's caught on well with the youth, who fell in love with the strong colors of the jackets and pants the company produced. In 1974, the use of such strong colors was daring and created the company image. Person's later expanded the use of its name to small household goods, and was even licensed to the Suzuki Automobile Company and applied to Suzuki motorcycles.

Person's initiated a new concept of DC (designer characters or designer name) brand products into the textile business; neither custom-made nor mass-produced, they are designed by experts and handcrafted. The products are marketed as a piece of the designer's character, a message from the designer to the user. They are relatively expensive to the buyer and much more profitable to the producer. By 1987, Person's had a capital of 700 million yen and held 180 subsidiaries, including those shops under direct management of Person's and those under a franchised system with independent management. The system protects the manufacturer from the pressure applied by large-scale retailers such as department stores to reduce prices, because the subsidiaries sell Person's products exclusively. It also enables the manufacturer to control the retail prices. Today, Person's has expanded by diversifying into restaurants, café bars, and galleries.

Atelier Sab, Inc. was started by Saburo Tanaka in 1976, originally making shirts and blouses for the spring and summer seasons, and leather products for the fall and winter seasons. In 1976, its total annual sales were already 450 million yen, rising to 630 million yen in 1977, one billion yen in 1978, 1.2 billion in 1979, and 1.4 billion by 1980. At that time, Tanaka decided to change the company policy. He gradually withdrew his products from the regular retail shops with which he had had long-standing relationships, and established his own subsidiaries to sell the products. In 1982, the number of subsidiaries increased, and the number of sales did too: 2 billion yen with seventeen subsidiary retail shops in 1983, 2.5 billion with forty-five shops in 1984, 4 billion with seventy-eight shops in 1985, and 13 billion with 160 shops by 1986.[9]

Person's and Atelier Sab are not exceptional in their upward growth from the periphery to the mainstream. The following fashion companies, once well outside the mainstream, are also now established as large and prestigious manufacturers: Atelier Nicol by Mitsuhiro Matsuda begun in 1967, Bigi Group in 1970, Issei Miyake International in 1971, Kansai Yamamoto in 1971, Yoji Yamamoto in 1972, and Comme de Garçon by Rei Kawakubo in 1973. Otsuka divides these companies into two groups: those which initially developed as externalizations of the artistic desires of designers, and those which were intended to develop commercially from their beginnings. Nicol and Bigi, as examples of the latter group, sold their products exclusively at their subsidiaries or their franchised shops in order to avoid the interference in their business of large retailers. They drew their employees from the younger generation that showed great enthusiasm for their products. The fans of Nicol and Bigi became the sale clerks who pushed their favorite merchandise, thus creating more fans. Those clerks were trained by the companies and sent to the retail shops under the special title of *hausu manukan* (house mannequins).[10]

More precisely, a top executive at Bigi explained to me that the organizational structure of Bigi consists, aside from the 200 working at headquarters, of about 2,000 to 2,500 people working in the 300 retail shops that sell Bigi products exclusively. These shops are under the direct management of Bigi headquarters. In addition, Bigi's products are sold through 700 franchised shops that operate under legal contract under a larger umbrella of Bigi "family." Western practices of legal contract, overlaid on the traditional system of quasi-family relationships in Japan, have created today's Japanese companies.

Although Bigi is in the category of having been commercialized from the beginning, the executive is fully aware of the creative side of his business. He says, "Fashion depends on popularity of the moment. If we do not catch up with the demand of the age, we will go out of business. We must always be creative. At the same time, it is important to keep a good balance between production and sales. They must be kept fifty-fifty. We should not indulge in creation." Endorsing Otsuka's point, he adds, "Seventeen years ago, when we started with only five employees, including myself, we had only one brand, Bigi. But now we have twenty brands, including Bigi. We have a new target among the youth between eighteen and twenty-three. For them, we sell products under the brand names Moga and Just Bigi, based on the new concept of designer characters."

Ten years ago, designer characters (DC) products were manufactured by only thirty companies. Today there are at least 600. The companies are often small, with only one designer and one partner, occupying an apartment room as office-factory. As a single apartment room is ironically called a "mansion" in Japan, these small producers have been named "mansion-makers." Now, it is harder than it used to be for a mansion-maker to find retail outlet shops in downtown Tokyo, as the market has been monopolized by the larger designer characters manufacturers. The mansion-makers have found markets in the towns that compose the residential belt surrounding Tokyo. After establishing retail relationships with about one hundred shops, business will start to flow steadily. The pure profit of a mansion-maker can be as high as ten percent of the sales; the margin of profitability is best when the annual sales range between 300–500 million yen. Beyond this, the risks increase. A company tends to lose it subsidiaries, spawning new companies.[11] Often a big manufacturer of designer's character products forms a group that contains subgroups organized in a hierarchy; each subgroup is managerially independent but usually under the control of the manufacturer who supplies the designer characters products under a specific brand name or names.

Staying Small and Powerful

In contrast to the cases described above, the current growth of individualism and entrepreneurship has added new momentum to the cycle from the periphery to the mainstream. The Bigi manager expressed his worry that the further expansion of his business may reduce creativity. He, like many others in the fashion industry, sees a large operation as a liability in the constantly changing world of fashion. Otsuka believes that the upper limit of an efficient company should be 500 million yen operating capital. Beyond that, a manufacturer must institute a change in management style, and in doing so begin to shift towards the establishment.

Akiko Arai, the owner of a fabric-design company, is an individualist. Against this shift, answering my questions, she replied, "I respect individuality. And to maintain my individuality, I prefer to be small. I would not be able to maintain individuality in a large company. I tried, and I gave up. To be large, I would have to appeal to the masses, and this means putting group cooperation before individual creativity. Besides, the struggle with the management of a large company was just exhausting." "However," she continues, "I do not wish to go against the establishment. What is most important is to be myself, but at the same time, 'compassion' is necessary. I create designs that will be easy to wear and easy to sell. It is compassion," she says, "and individuality and compassion are compatible." She speaks in favor of the youth with individualistic tendencies, although she does not like labeling them New Men.

Kimiko Murata (pseudonym), the daughter of the owner of a high-quality shoe manufacturing company, designs shoes for her father and has already taken over part of his business. She is proud of being "established small," to supply only a limited quantity of high-quality and fashionable shoes to a limited market. Her complaint is that her original designs were constantly being stolen and copied by larger manufacturing companies. In fact, I later did find many shoes similar to her designs being sold at much lower prices. Murata values creativity and originality greatly; she also says, "New Men are great, as long as they insist on their uniqueness, which no one else in Japan does so explicitly." She pointed out some qualities that she feels New Men should have: a sense of responsibility, common sense, and "coolness."

In another peripheral area of the economy, Kiyoto Otani (pseudonym) heads a real estate firm. Otani began his life as a "marginal" Japanese, having lived abroad between the ages of five and ten. When he returned to Japan, he spoke very little Japanese. Yet within several years, he advanced from the bottom to the very top of his class. After he graduated from the prestigious Keio University, he opted to remain outside the group, earning his master's degree in business at Harvard University. Although the real estate business ranks low on the social prestige scale, unless one's company is extremely large, Otani keeps his firm small. He is proud and determined to be self-reliant and on the periphery.

Ichikazu Yanagida, the owner of a small but innovative company in the high-tech industry, holds that all members of a company should be able "to ride on a single bus."

Otherwise, the owner of the company cannot give good care to the workers or appreciate their work individually. When this size limit is adhered to, the management is automatically concentrated in the owner-president of the company. Yanagida asserts that the diffusion of management, resulting also in a depletion of human resources as a strength in a company, marks the beginning of corruption. The president must know every worker in his company.

According to Yanagida, "staying small" in the high-tech industry has definite merit. His creative company does not manufacture products, but only designs them. Material products are made on a contractual basis by other companies that are better geared for manual labor. He says that the design and development of one product requires twenty designers, who all can ride on the same bus, but manufacturing the same product requires an additional 200 workers, too many for any one bus or for efficient management. Although Yanigada emphasizes the importance of creativity and the development of new ideas, he is reluctant to sell raw ideas. The practical reason for this is that the Japanese are willing to buy products, but not yet accustomed to pay for thoughts. From the consumer's point of view, buying the finished product is preferable because the designers take direct responsibility for it. In this respect, his company policy is different from larger companies, which now anticipate an even greater separation of concepts and products in the future.

Yanagida also emphasizes that he is not an exception and that there are many like him who are running small businesses. He believes that they should develop in antithesis to the established economic culture. The development of more of these new-style businesses could break the group orientation and its rigid hierarchies. The contrast between how individual and group creativity are defined in companies will be significant in determining the countenance of Japan's future economic culture. Yanagida, unlike mainstream groupists, has no complaints about the youth. He says that they quickly make clear choices; when they show interest in what he offers them, he can expect their full commitment to his production. Possibly, New Men may do much better under individualistic managers outside the mainstream groupism than working within the mainstream culture.

Small Production in Large Variety

The creative industry's policy of "staying small" under individualistic management fits in well in the new age of small production/ large variety.

Toshio Sanuki, an economist speaking at the Symposium for New Business, predicted the development of the market in the near future:

> I have estimated how the world market will expand in 2000 A.D. Supposing that the economic growth holds constant at the rate of 3.5%, a 217 trillion yen new market could be created for the next 15 years. This will be 1.55 trillion dollars. . . . This means that a new market will be as large as the total of the three developed markets in Europe today, namely the British, French and West

German. The question is whether this large new market will contribute equally to all industries and firms. The answer is *no*. Industries based on the traditional technology will grow as little as 6% in the next 15 years. However, industries based on highly developed technology could develop twenty-eight times as large as those we have now.[12]

Professor Hajime Karatsu, of Tokai University, speaking at the same symposium, emphasized the importance of applied technology:

What is most important in the high-tech area is developed in terms of use. . . . When a new technology is created in the West, the Westerners wish to apply it to high-grade purposes such as airplanes, missiles, and space development. These areas are already difficult enough without further complication by the development of new technology. The Japanese are different. When carbon fibers were invented, the first application was in black-shaft mass-production. After stable quality and low costs had been achieved, the fibers began to be used in the airplane production. . . . Another example is form-memory amalgam. In Japan it was first used in coffee makers, air conditions, and Wacor's brassieres. Although I do not really know the importance since I am a man, brassieres must be kept in shape even when they are stored. It was difficult to achieve, but the Wacor bras are now fine. At regular temperatures, they expand into desired shape. I think this was a great invention. As a result, ninety percent of form-memory amalgam products are made in Japan.[13]

Sanuki claims that what he and his generation have been producing manually will be made by robots in the near future, thus lowering the cost of production. However, in order to meet the demand for small quantity/large variety, mass-produced merchandise will have to be finished up in small or intermediate-sized factories to add finer differentiations. Each item is produced and sold in an extremely short-term market. The robot used here will have to be, accordingly, made more flexible. New designer and manufacturing areas should be explored to develop replaceable or revisable robots. Sanuki also suggests that users should collaborate with manufacturers to create products that will more closely meet consumers' demands. The products must be finely differentiated, so that each displays a unique character.

From the viewpoint of smaller manufacturers, Sanuki's predictions sound like glad tidings. However, they carry with them problems of implementation. Large and established companies have been integrating smaller manufacturers, as subcontractors, into the bottom strata of their organizations. Under tight and exclusive control of the larger companies, inferior work conditions have been imposed. This fate is widely feared by smaller and entrepreneurial business. At all costs, they would like to avoid becoming subcontractors; yet at the same time they are aware that their status as independent producers limits their competitive edge. The ability required to survive under such constraints dispels any notion that individualistic entrepreneurs are "spoiled kids" or "flower children" in the milieu of today's economic prosperity. They have chosen to stay on the periphery as a way to realize their goals in the future, and they have accepted that insecurity is a necessary condition for the freedom to pursue their experiments.

Notes

1. Toshinao Yoneyama (1976) argues for endorsing Shibata's personal experience on a wider scale of application.
2. Statistics Bureau of the Management and Coordination Agency of the Japanese Government, 1988.
3. Tokyo Keizai Weekly, 1987, p. 6.
4. Ibid., p. 9.
5. Ibid., p. 12.
6. Ibid., p. 5.
7. Ministry of Labor, 1987, p. 116.
8. Moritani, 1987, p. 22.
9. Otsuka, 1987, pp. 22-3, 14-5.
10. Ibid., pp. 14-5.
11. Ibid., p. 31.
12. Japan Future Society 1987, p. 169.
13. Ibid., p. 127.

3

From Subculture to Antithesis

Cold Reality

The large and elite businesses that are well-known for their group orientation and lifetime employment system constitute less than one percent of all businesses in Japan. They employ only twenty percent of the nation's working population, including blue-collar workers, and produce about sixty percent of products in Japan.[1] Of all the businesses in Japan, 99.3 percent are officially categorized as either "small" or "intermediate."[2] Despite the fact that they make up the majority of the economy, such companies and their employees are regarded as socially "marginal." They offer neither security not prestige, are less productive per capita, and are more or less subject to legal protection. In contrast to elites, they are commonly described negatively and have not been appreciated in their own right.

Figures published by the Ministry of Labor indicate that compared to large businesses, small and intermediate ones suffer in a number of aspects. One is the disparity in wages. In 1986, manufacturing businesses with 500 or more workers paid an average wage of 381,700 yen a month; those with only five to twenty-nine workers paid an average of 212,800 yen.[3] In addition, the workers in small businesses work longer hours. There is also an inverse relationship between the size of the business and the number of work hours. The larger the business is, the fewer hours employees work.[4]

Typically, the statistics on work hours compiled by the Ministry of Labor ignore those businesses with fewer than five workers. In such small businesses, the work hours are usually long and erratic. The statistics on monthly wages take into account only businesses with ten or more workers. Those with fewer often have workers living in their factories, and room and board is including in their wages, thus reducing their cash wages. In an effort to provide psychological compensations to make up for such inferior working conditions, very small businesses often cultivate a stronger sense of family than is found in the large, "family-oriented" companies in the mainstream.

A Trap for Entrepreneurs

Subcontracting is a large issue among smaller manufacturers. Out of the approximately 710,000 small businesses in Japan, 65.5 percent, or 465,000 are subcontractors under the control of larger corporations.[5] The textile and machine manufacturing industries show the highest percentage of subcontractors, averaging 80 percent of this segment, or which over 50 percent have only one to three workers.[6]

In Japanese society, subcontractors develop a special bond with larger businesses. On the surface, the subcontractor's status is legally defined and codified in such away that the subcontractor provides parts and services to the larger company.[7] However, in addition to this rationalized relationship, there is another parallel relationship which more faithfully reflects the ideological interpretation and application of the quasi-kinship idioms essential in Japanese society. The two businesses enter into a quasi-parent-child relationship, and in doing so, develop a permanent and exclusive bond. The child organization becomes a family member of the parent company. For example, a subcontractor who works exclusively for Sony will consider himself to be a part of Sony. The parts the subcontractor produces are, in fact, all used in Sony products and become Sony's. However, the parts made by subcontractors are less profitable, subject to fast model changes, and more labor-intensive than those produced in-house. In addition, these products must undergo rigid quality control by the parent corporation. It is common practice for a large company to have more than several layers of subcontractors: the direct subcontractors, relatively large, hire a layer of sub-subcontractors; this second layer produces a third, and so on. During a period of recession, the bottom layer tends to be the first to be dropped from the hierarchy. This risk-absorption mechanism ensures the security of the lifetime employees in the parent companies, reinforcing their elite status, and it perpetuates security as a component of prestige in the social structure.

Under these conditions, subcontractors do not enjoy legal protection or clear-cut rights in arbitration disputes, as they would in a truly modern and democratic system. In the quasi-parent-child relationship, where loyalty and emotional bonds are essential, taking a problem to court entails the end of the relationship itself. To preserve the relationship, problems must be solved through a harmonious negotiation process, in which both parties must avoid acting offensively or even directly presenting the problem. If a dispute cannot be resolved in this way, the government intervenes as a mediator,[8] invoking laws and regulations as guidelines for negotiation, but not for making judgements. In this way, the laws and regulations are used not to define the limits of power that the parent company holds over the child subcontractor, but rather to set the terms and standards for negotiation. Therefore, the way in which the laws are employed serves less to protect than to maintain the subjugation of the child companies.

For example, the "Law Concerning the Prevention of Delayed Payment in Commissional Contracts"[9] stipulates that the parent corporation must pay its bill to the child corporation within sixty days after the delivery of goods, indicating that payment is rarely made before sixty days after delivery. Other "legally" prohibited actions include the enforcement of excessively low prices and the return of unsold merchandise to the child corporations, leading to the assumption that such actions are common. The continuation of a contract after the agreed conditions have lapsed is also subject to governmental mediation.[10] The existence of these guidelines may improve the situation of the subcontractor, but by no means does it give it rights equal to those of the parent corporation.

Restructuring Economic Relations

Some small businesses have made an effort to remain independent without subcontracting to larger firms. They have begun to
develop a unity and cooperative relationships among themselves. If
they are successful, alliances of smaller businesses will be able to
achieve social positions that are more equal and complementary in
relation to larger businesses. Sanuki's suggestions for cooperation
between large and small manufacturers also have a greater chance
to become real, if relationships between smaller and larger businesses become more contractual and less dependent on the traditional quasi-kinship ideology. However, the general reaction to
attempts on the part of smaller businesses to achieve a competitive
position relative to larger businesses has been negative. In response
to my inquiries, a consultant working for Techno-Information and
Communications Center (TICC), a subdivision of the Association
for Smaller Businesses,[11] expressed his doubt about such possibilities. In his opinion, creative smaller businesses have good ideas but
have difficulty in merchandising them. Most smaller businesses lack
the expertise to successfully market their newly-developed products. Although TICC tries to teach these business skills, the owners
of small businesses, although they may be good inventors, do not
always make good businessmen.

Ichikazu Yanagida, the owner of a small high-tech company,
recognizes this difficulty and has come up with a proposal to
overcome it. He has developed a new model of small business
alliance, an association giving each member equal status. Although
his model emphasizes the importance of group dynamics and human resources as much as the mainstream values them, it departs
from traditional groupists in its incorporation of equal status for
group members. His association would function as a think tank
including the owners of independent companies, each of whom
would contribute his own specialized knowledge and skills.

Yanagida says, "For example, when I receive an order to create
a sensor to check the quality of a final electrical appliance product
mass-produced in a large factory, I need to cooperate with specialists in five different fields to create the sensor." Under his proposal,
instead of hiring five specialists for his company, Yanagida would

be able to draw upon an association of specialists from different fields who could share their diverse talents.

Structural Determinants

Yanagida's proposal is significant because of its basis in giving its members equal status. It is intentionally antithetical to the hierarchical social organization of traditional Japanese groups in the mainstream. The specific character of human relationships is particularly important in any analysis of Japanese society, as it is recognized that these relationships are the structural determinants of the cohesion of Japanese society. Not only is there an academic consensus about its importance, but the experience of foreign business people who have learned to successfully interact in Japanese society, in the Japanese economic market, and who have realized that understanding Japanese human relationships is essential, has also served to strengthen agreement on this point.

In the modern culture of technology of Japan, the traditional relationships have been conceptualized according to a "vertical principle" that ignores the structural pluralism and "horizontal" forms of relationships which have existed traditionally.[12] The first structural analysis of Japanese groupism was conducted by Chie Nakane, a British-trained anthropologist. She schematized the structure of Japanese group relationships into a vertical principle, based on observation of the male-dominated workplace. Her theory was later supported by her own study of rural households in northern Japan.

Nakane's concept of the vertical principle clarifies the internal structure of the Japanese group. It explains, at the same time, why Japanese groups do not allow individualistic participants. She describes a typical Japanese group as an accumulation of quasi-parent-child relationships, the relationship between subcontractor and larger businesses being one variation on this theme. One of her major points is that dyadic bonds among group members are always formed vertically, that is, hierarchically:

As has been said, the group is based on the accumulation of relationships between two individuals: the group . . . consists of the relationships a-b, a-c, b-d, b-e, c-f, c-g. The relationship between two individuals of upper and lower status is the basis of the structural principle of Japanese society. This important relationship is expressed in the traditional terms *oyabun* and *kobun*. *Oyabun* means the person with the status of *oya* (parent) and *kobun* means with the status of *ko* (child) . . . b is the *kobun* of a *oyabun*, and at the same time he is the *oyabun* of d. One person may play more than one role. The traditional *oyabun-kobun* relationship took this form.[13]

In brief, Nakane describes a Japanese group as a hierarchical and pyramidic network of numerous-pair bonds created between a superior and an inferior, but *not* between equals.

The membership of the group is traditionally limited. Members are expected to maintain a lifelong relationship to their own group. The members of hierarchical pair relationships weave an intimacy with their unequal partners over the passage of time, the relationship becoming personalized, custom-made and unique to each pair. Two unequal partners develop a close and emotionally involving relationship similar to that of parent and child, and, once this relationship has been built and shared, it continues forever, like a kinship bond. The participants are not given the choice of staying or leaving the relationship. Thus, the internal structure of Japanese groups necessarily enforces closedness and emotional involvement in its members. The lifetime employment system has provided a convenient framework for sustaining these patterns.

Becoming a Self-Validating Theory

When Nakane first published her daring theory in 1968, it was intended solely as an objective analysis:

I approach this issue through a structural analysis, not a cultural or historical explanation. The working of what I call the vertical principle in Japanese society is the theme of this book. In my view, the most characteristic feature of Japanese social organization arises from the single bond in social relationships: an individual or a group has always one single distinctive relation to the other. The working of this kind of relationship meets the unique structure of Japanese society as a whole, which contrasts to that of caste or class societies. Thus Japanese values are manifested. Some of my Japanese readers might feel repelled in the face of some parts of my discussion; where I expose certain Japanese weaknesses they might even feel considerable distaste. I do this, however, not because of a hypocritical view of the Japanese or Japanese life but because I intend to be as objective as possible in this analysis of the society to which I belong. I myself take these weaknesses for granted as elements which constitute part of the entire body which also has its great strengths.[14]

In the same year, Japan's economy provided the second highest gross national product per capita in the free economic world. The increasing role of international finance and trade exposed many unwilling Japanese to the conflicts, confrontations, and crises inherent in extended contact with other cultures. The situation demanded that the Japanese invent ways to survive the turmoil of such confrontations of other cultural values with their own. A common solution was not to face cultural and value diversities by individualizing themselves, but to solidify their group unity against Western individualists. In this response, in fact, the Japanese proudly proclaimed their own uniqueness lay. They built their modern economy on collectivity, one of the basic traditional values. Many leading Japanese hold the assumption that the contemporary national character has been achieved at the cost of increasing isolationism, the upholding of a sense of uniqueness shared only by the Japanese among themselves. That is, groupism founded upon the vertical principle is an extension of Japanese tradition, and the contemporary sense of Japanese uniqueness is founded upon the defense of traditional values against Westernization. This assumption is the major impetus behind the force of nationalism in the modern culture of technology.

Nakane's theory, in spite of her assertions that her analysis was meant to be objective, was adopted by those Japanese in the mainstream to justify their group ethic and promoted by many writers in popular cultural analyses. Their writings have strengthened the popular acceptance in Japan of the social values that define the modern culture of technology. These writers used Nakane's theory to promote and establish groupism and nationalism, and mainstream social organizations took on their coloration via her formulations. Her observations were used to codify the structure of group relations and were, in a sense, reduced to a self-validating theory. As the vertical principle was agreed to be the essential component of Japanese society, it was commonly characterized as the "society of vertical principle." By definition groups which did not fit into Nakane's theory as it was interpreted have come to be considered deviant. Yet by adopting this limited version of Nakane's theory, the modern culture of technology has failed to account for the structural pluralism that is an active component of today's Japan, and it has also failed to acknowledge the horizontal ties present in Japanese human relationships.

Cross-Organizational Relationships

In Nakane's model, pairs of relationships develop only vertically or hierarchically, and only in one's group. In reality, however, pairs of relationships also develop horizontally into a private friendship network outside of the group, through one-on-one contact and without formal grouping. The network develops cross-organizationally, informally combining people who formally belong to different groups. This type of network, functioning typically in business, is dependent on another custom commonly known as *nemawashi*. The literal meaning of *nemawashi* is "to bind the roots with a rope for transplantation," a horticultural technique not known to Americans until it was introduced there by Japanese gardeners. Westerners were surprised to see the Japanese transplanting large trees without damaging their roots, by digging a hole around the tree and binding the roots before transplanting it. As the rope binds the roots in the soil, the roots are tightly contained in the "pot" made of rope. The tree is transferred and planted in the rope pot. As time goes on, the rope rots, allowing new roots to grow through it. Finally, the rope even fertilizes the tree.

Figuratively, in Japan root-binding means to lobby people in different social organizations, before any formal or legal gestures taken place. The root-binding process begins far in advance of formal negotiations over a legal contract. The very first step is building a communication channel to the other group. A person in Group A tries to discuss the possibility of future business with a person from Group B. At this level of development, no matter how concrete and realistic the discussion may appear, it is simply "talk." Often, this social interaction is aided by the consumption of alcohol, and thus may flow into fantasy. Through repeated meetings, the two persons develop a standard Japanese intimate pair relationship. This time, however, the relationship is formed "horizontally" as a friendship and not "vertically" between a superior and an inferior.

The importance of developing such cross-organizational relationships motivates the Japanese to seek to expand their private reservoir of relationships to people outside their own organization. If a person in a given organization already has a friend or an acquaintance in another, it is convenient for the development of other new relationships. For the same reasons, keeping friends in many different organizations increases one's private resources. The strongest base for such horizontal relationships is a former friendship: two people who were once members of the same group, childhood playmates, former classmates from any level of education, present or past members of the same club. The importance of attending the right school is evident in the role such ties play. Attendance at prestigious schools leads to placement in major firms, and once established at a company, a person will find his former classmates distributed among various organizations, creating excellent networking opportunities. As a company man, he is secure in his own organization and does not need to compete with his friends in different organizations, so he is free to be extremely open and intimate in his private relationships with them. Ronald Dore describes this situation well:

> The British electrician is assumed to need a strong local and national organization to ensure that the skills of electricians are given their proper price, and that work which should go to electricians is not given to others—and that requires defining both what is electrician's work and who should be entitled to call himself an electrician. He shares his concern for these things equally with other electricians in other firms. An electrician working for Hitachi probably did not become an electrician until he passed out of the labor market into Hitachi. Once in the firm he is never likely to go into the market again to sell his electrician skills and so he has no particular interest in keeping up their price. Within the firm, given the wage system, his interests coincide rather more with those of non-electricians of the same age as himself than with those of older or younger fellow electricians.[15]

Dore also points out an interesting example of a section chief creating pressure on his own company:

> although there is no individual bargaining pressure to raise salaries there is what might be called dispersed collective pressure. A section chief in the personnel

department—who has the records—will compute the average salary for section chiefs at various levels of seniority, and swap the information informally with his opposite numbers in the three other big electrical firms. If it turns out that Hitachi comes badly out of comparison, the word will spread around and individual section chiefs will send the message up through their immediate superiors that there are certain obvious remedial measures which would visibly enhance their sense of dedication to Hitachi.[16]

Thus, traditional relationships, when developed horizontally and cross-organizationally, function to exchange services, information, and goods. Goods are given to compensate for the provision of services and information. They are also exchanged during the two gift-giving seasons, year-end and midsummer, further renewing the bonds between donor and recipient. As part of this practice, the exchange of New Year greeting cards is indispensable and an important tool in maintaining contacts. Cards with standardized messages and illustrations are sent to friends and acquaintances; any gestures to personalize the cards are appreciated by their recipients. As the number of people in a private network expands endlessly, one may easily send and receive over one hundred, and even over a thousand, cards for each season. As long as a person sends a card and receives one in return, he is assured of a lifetime network contact. Whenever necessity arises, help can be requested from the most desirable contact among the large group of acquaintances.

The Horizontal Principle

As a private resource, a horizontal network of friends commonly functions through go-betweens. The necessity of go-betweens is the result of the very nature of structural pluralism, where every social organization develops its own defining culture for its members. The following example, taken from my field notes, reveals a typical function of the horizontal principle, where (a) in group A and (b) in group B become known to each other through (c), a go-between.

It should be noted that this example is deliberately chosen from outside the work situation, in order to show that the horizontal network is deeply traditional and practiced by everyone in Japanese society. *Nemawashi* is an application of this tradition in today's modern culture of technology. In the following example, (a) is the mother of a primary school child and (b) is the president of the Parent Teacher Association of the school to which the mother (a) wants to transfer her son. (c) is a close friend of (a) who attended that primary school with (b). The story runs as follows: A mother had a son who had disagreed with his teacher, who wanted all of the children in her class to act exactly according to her instruction. No deviation from the given instructions was allowed, and any deviation that occurred was extremely disturbing to her. In her eyes, the son was restless and unfit in the class.

The mother telephoned all her friends (in her horizontal friendship network), one after another, telling them that she wanted to transfer her son to a particular school that was known for giving students more flexibility. Concidentally, she found that a close friend, now a teacher, had attended this school as a child. In addition, the president of the Parent Teacher Association at the new school was one of this friend's former classmates.

This situation typically requires a friend to act as a go-between. She (c) stood between her two friends, the mother (a) and the president (b), who did not know each other. The mother had found a go-between in her private resource of friendship. According to the horizontal principle, she was entitled to take advantage of her friend in solving her problem. Her friend the go-between, further following the horizontal principle, introduced the mother to the Parent Teacher Association president, who took the mother to the school and introduced her to the principal of the school. At first, the transfer did not seem possible. This particular school was a public school and did not usually accept children from outside of its district. However, the school had recently convinced the local Board of Education to allow it to accept a few transfer students, as its attendance by children in the district had been decreasing, due to development of the area. The Board of Education had long intended to try to close the school by cutting its budget, and the school itself had wanted to stay open by filling its student vacancies with children outside the district. The situation was complicated, although both the principal and the Parent Teacher Association president were sympathetic to the mother who wanted to transfer her child.

The mother became annoyed and discouraged. Nothing was moving in the right direction. She was told by the local government office that she should wait until the next academic year, rather than transferring her son in the middle of the year. However, she thought that her son would not be able to keep up with the heavy study load under his present teacher, and that by the beginning of the next academic year he would truly not fit into the educational system.

Her friend was knowledgeable about the academic system and the attitude of those in the local school administration. She suggested that the mother meet with the administrators involved as often as possible, to impress them with her dedication as a mother. At first, the mother hesitated, thinking that this might appear too aggressive and alienate the administrators. Eventually, she took the advice of her friend, and her son was transferred.

The friend made an effort to explain to the mother what the orientation of the local school administration was. The primary school in question was located in a downtown commercial area, where people traditionally appreciate straightforwardness. In this community, the mother could push a long way without offending people. However, she had no way of knowing this until her friend informed her. Because the framework of structural pluralism enforces group isolationism, the friend was the only one who knew how things operated in both groups. The friend, as a go-between, in place of the mother, also had to convince the president of the Parent Teacher Association that both parents were good citizens and that their son was a good child in spite of his teacher's negative evaluation. Her familiarity with the parents lent force and sincerity to her appeal on their behalf.[17]

In today's society, the pervasive myth of cultural homogeneity, obstructing the awareness of structural pluralism, has added a difficulty to the role of the go-between; believing that the other party will act and think in the same way they do, it takes awhile for the average Japanese to realize that "We, the Japanese" are not all the same.

New Attempts

On the periphery, there are active attempts to take advantage of horizontal relationships. Entrepreneurs in the high-tech industry organize associations which function to unite smaller companies with different skills. Ichikazu Yanagida came up with an idea: he cooperates with his friends in the different high-tech areas to create new products. He believes that technological development proceeds at a furious speed today, and that large corporations established on the vertical principle are too rigid and inflexible to adjust to rapidly changing markets. Being small is a definite advantage, as consumers constantly demand personalized products and services. The lack of production capacity can be overcome by cooperation among small companies. By cooperating on a basis of equal status, the owners of smaller companies maintain independence from each other, and a fairly large association based on this kind of relationship can be competitive enough to prevent subcontracting under larger companies.

Yanagida emphasizes that by creating such alternative horizontal organizations, the risks for peripheral businesses will be diffused and more efficiently absorbed. This represents a new version of tradition continuing in the modern economy.

There is another experiment taking place, based on the horizontal principle. Yanagida is the leader of the Yokohama Venture Business Club, in Yokohama, a city adjacent to Tokyo, where many small high-tech companies are located. Venture Business Clubs, local clubs of entrepreneurs in the high-tech industry, form a nationwide network organized as Technological Exchange Plazas. Yanagida invited me to a "business-cards exchange party" in order to show how his club functions. The party was held in his office suite and there was an admission fee of 2,000 yen. Beer, cocktails, coffee, and snacks were served. After fifty people came, introducing themselves first to the party in general and then individually to one another by exchanging their business cards. Most were owners or top executives of high-tech companies and consultants specializing in high technology. There were a few people from the Ministry of Trade and Industry, and a few ambitious young people from large and established companies. The young people enthusiastically collected information and made inquiries about possible business connections.

Such parties are held on a regular basis and attract new faces in addition to established members. In this way, the Venture Clubs function in a role similar to the go-between in the traditional horizontal relationship. Members are expected to take advantage of the part to recruit each other into their own horizontal networks. The clubs and their activities represent another version of tradition revised and modernized.

Yanagida is critical of authorities such as government officials, university professors, and other self-proclaimed opinion leaders of the modern culture of technology in Japan, who try to keep such horizontal organization under their control. He insists that horizontal networking is still a private resource and has room for development in many directions, and that it should be kept "purposely ambiguous" and free of such control. In spite of opposition to the authorization of horizontal relationships, such as Yanagida's criticism, the Japanese government has been trying to unify local business clubs into larger and more formal organizations, under a policy of "managerial resource combination." Conceivably, this could lead to the exchange, combination, coordination, and interlinking of business areas formerly held separate or considered incompatible. New technologies, new products, new businesses, and even new consumer demands could emerge from such recombinations, and there is the expectation that producers would be stimulated to break existing boundaries, both in practice and in theory.

New products created from the joint efforts of different businesses will attract the attention of consumers, tired of seeing the same goods in the same shops.[18] This kind of horizontal cooperation is particularly important for smaller businesses, as without a self-supporting network, they are more liable to buyouts or recruitment into larger firms as subcontractors. As the vocational and academic backgrounds of the owners of smaller companies vary greatly, their informal networks do not efficiently overlap in the same way as those of executives of larger companies who are usually from the same top universities. The exchanges among smaller businesses, therefore, will not be simple unifications of managerial resources but the creation of new business areas through a kind of cross-pollination. Once smaller businesses relate to each other as active partners, more entrepreneurial and more creative activities should emerge—small in scale but full of new ideas.

The consultant at Techno-Information and Communication Center (TICC) responded to my inquiries by saying that "the government is taking taxes from larger businesses to promote smaller businesses, despite their rivalry in the market." In addition to preparing what is tentatively called the "Law Concerning the Unification of Small and Intermediate Businesses," more financial aid will be provided through the Association for Smaller Businesses (Chusho Kigyo Jigyo Dan). The total budget requested for 1988 was 244.3 billion yen, a 6.9 percent increase over 1987. The government is also prepared to aid in the development of new businesses, with a 500 million yen budget that is equally shared by the national and the prefectural government, a tax exemption for the membership fee of joining the business unification process for the development of new businesses, low interest loans, and insurance policies to absorb risks for developing new businesses.[19]

TICC keeps in close contact with the Technology Exchange Plazas, to exchange information and technology for smaller businesses all over Japan. The Plazas are formed at the local, seminational, and national levels. For 10,000 yen, they provide members with the membership roster and a quarterly newsletter reporting technological and economic developments, and helps members obtain more detailed information on subjects it reports on. Application for membership in the national-level exchange plaza, the National Association for the Exchange among Different Businesses, must be made by a group of five or more businesses. This requirement prevents the National Association from having to deal with each small business separately, and it avoids any overlap in function with the local Plaza, which numbered 94 in 1987.[20]

The Association for Smaller Businesses, of which TICC is a subdivision, trains mediators, officially called "catalyzers" ("kataraiza"), at the College of Small and Intermediate Businesses, and sends them to Plazas to accelerate the process of unifying different businesses. This is another attempt to take advantage of the traditional role of go-betweens who bring together individuals from different groups.

A young official of the Ministry of Trade and Industry whom I interviewed was optimistic about the future of smaller businesses. He appreciated their spirit of entrepreneurship and said that their growing strength is important for the future of Japan. According to him, although he emphasized that many businesses do meet the requirements, the selection of financial aid recipients is a strict process. At one time, aid was given to any small business wanting to expand; today candidates must prove that they have the capacity to expand and must pass a series of examinations.

Counterresponse by the Establishment

While an active appreciation of individualism remains character-istic of the periphery culture, it has threatened the mainstream to the degree that the mainstream has had to adapt itself to changing conditions in the modern economy. Large mainstream corporations established on groupism still maintain high production levels, but in order to keep their market leadership position, they must invest in new ventures. This is particularly true of the high-tech industry, whose investments today are in applied science, but who also must look toward pure science, which will create tomorrow's markets. Large groupist companies, however, have difficulty in retaining creative scientists in their firms. These types of individuals love their freedom. Companies fear that they may lose them to the allures of the periphery, and they offer special privileges, in addi-tion to security and prestige, in order to try to keep such individuals in the company.

I met with the directors of the high-tech Nippon Electric Com-pany (NEC), who gave me some insights into the firm. In 1969, NEC systematically researched its wages and salaries, in order to match wages more accurately with variations in individual abilities.

This was one year after Japan's gross national product per capita became the second highest in the free world, and expectations for social changes were high. At NEC, about 140 people were involved in the one-year analysis and construction of the new wage system, with the full cooperation of the NEC labor union. As a result, a new wage system was established based on a combination of seniority and meritocracy. The resulting modified lifetime employ-ment system, or "establishment meritocracy," was adopted by others and is now quite common.

Later, NEC adopted a bilateral promotion system called the Dual

Ladder System. Among regular employees, promotion means advancement to a supervisory position. Researchers, however, are neither good at nor interested in management. Thus, to keep them content and productive, their promotion is advancement with no obligation to management. At the inception of the system, NEC copied the American model, calling such researchers "fellows," and emphasizing their independence from the traditional order of positions based on seniority. However, soon the system was adjusted to conform more to the hierarchical lifetime employment system.

The major difference between NEC's and the most common American system is that in Japan the system provided the opportunity for upward mobility primarily within the confines of the company, whereas the American system factors upward mobility with the variable of providing coping mechanisms (such as monetary incentives) to deal with the possibility that employees will choose to leave the company. NEC is well aware that the possibility of losing quality workers to other companies is becoming greater in today's social milieu. But as drastic salary raises are not permitted under the seniority system, NEC tries to compensate by offering the best possible research facilities and conditions for its scientists. Even with the revisions based on "ability-ism," it is not possible within the society's framework for a person twenty-five years old to be earning three times as much as a person fifty years old. Instead, NEC offers research budgets of as much as a million dollars annually to one or two outstanding researchers. The scientists who are placed in the NEC Research Institute are allowed to pursue their own projects and areas of interest. The directors whom I interviewed were adamant that talented researchers are more concerned about their research than salaries, and that only under the lifetime employment system, without the pressures to come up with immediate results, can a long-term research project thrive. In fact, company researchers are rarely recruited away from their firms. The directors recalled only a few who have left to go to top universities, apparently because to them professorship was more prestigious than a position in private industry. Those researchers who remained at NEC thought their colleagues' decisions to leave unwise, because they had left an ideal research atmosphere for mere prestige.

NEC has developed its own theory of the process of creative research, called Group Creation. Under the system, a team of scientists and engineers are responsible for the development of a new product, from research to creation. Even though Group Creation begins its activities with the original idea of a particular researcher, there are not many of these researchers in the firm. Yet NEC's directors emphasized that they had the utmost confidence in the inventiveness of their researchers. They admitted that developing ideas into commercial products is almost always a group process. Although they agreed that the original researcher should remain responsible to the end of the process of production, in practice, when original concepts are transferred to a development division, the inventor's job is over, and he is usually not interested in the commercial phase of development.

In the fashion industry, large and established firms also employ a bilateral promotion system. Kazuyo Azuma (pseudonym) of Naigai, a top fabric and clothing company, told me that there is a clear distinction between creative and other personnel at Naigai. The creative staff are mostly designers, as she is, patterners, and graders, making up about 150 people, while another 2,500 are employed in manufacturing, sales, and administration. The majority are lifetime employees ranked according to seniority, with slight adjustments arrived at from individual ability evaluation. In contrast, the creative staff are evaluated solely on their ability and professional performance. They are not insured under lifetime employment. While bonuses, ranging from a half-month's to a few months' salary, are usually paid twice a year to lifetime employees, the creative staff receives no bonuses. They are all under one-year contracts, which do not give them a sense of security but do protect their mobility and freedom. For the same reason, retirement benefits are not given to creative staff; they are a privilege of lifetime employees, who receive at the time of retirement, as much as several hundred thousand dollars, depending on their positions in the company.

As a result, in Naigai, the creative staff operate under a semi-American system. Azuma said that it is important for designers to be persuasive and even argumentative. She says, "In the creative process of designing, I speak freely. My [male] boss exists in order to make my work easier. His task is not to make demands on me but to accommodate me for accomplishing my responsibilities." She continued, "Of course, I still feel frustrated in the male-dominant society, especially the male-dominated sales department, which, in general, operates on the vertical principle of Japanese society with the customers, thus creating closed markets based on closed and hierarchical human relationships."

Teruko Kobayashi, an artist whom I interviewed, feels comfortable in the mainstream. She has developed her administrative ability along with the expansion of Kose Company. The company started with a staff of six in 1946, one year after World War II ended. Teruko Kobayashi joined it in 1958. She was assigned to the Makeup Research Section in the Marketing Research Division. At first, she was a staff of one in her section. Staff were added, one after another, as the company expanded to become a top cosmetics manufacturer. Today, her title is "Total Beauty Director."

When I interviewed her, I realized that she is more of an artist than a businesswoman, although she has been extremely successful in sales. Under the management of Kose, her new concept of makeup, to which she is dedicated, has flourished. She says that she has been tempted to become independent a few times, but that she has not been able to find a better backer than Kose, which she feels honestly appreciates her unique ability to read future social currents and conceptualize trends as marketable products. Kose has appointed her principal of the Best Makeup School, newly built in downtown Tokyo.

Unlike the automotive and heavy steel industries, technological changes occur quickly in the fashion and high-tech industries. Because of this, the management of most of the fashion and high-tech companies do not enforce the Japanese work ethic over their creative staff. Some employ the dual ladder promotion system under "modified ability-ism," while others retain the formal life-time system. However, in both cases, a formal system is not enforced, as long as supervisors are convinced that staff members are coming up with creative innovations. As is apparent in Kobayashi's company and NEC, under lifetime employment, creative researchers are subject to only lenient and infrequent evaluation, and they may safely involve themselves in long-term experiments with a high degree of job security.

There is a common assumption that in order to be successful, one must be constantly driven by a fear of failure. Most Japanese, however, would insist that a person must be secure in order to concentrate creatively, and that fear of failure can disrupt concentration. Many, either Japanese or non-Japanese, would agree that a fear of failure itself can lead to failure. In Japan, security is another name given to prestige, a major privilege achieved by becoming a member of the elite. In contrast, in America, security is often associated with lack of ambition or imagination.

On the periphery, owners of creative firms, in contrast to mainstream elites, are under pressure. They could be swept out in an economic crisis, and consequently must be sharply business-minded as well as creative. Yet because they are small, they are more flexible and can respond more quickly to social change; they are less burdened with orthodox social values. They can more easily gain top management positions, available to only a few under the mainstream seniority system. The owners of smaller companies may take more chances and face more insecurity, but they may also enjoy a greater kind of security than some in the mainstream. Their very independence gives them a kind of security in the knowledge of self-determination and self-realization in their products. Despite these differences, what is significant now is that creative interaction is developing between the periphery and the mainstream.

Notes

1. Shoko Chukin, 1987, p. 1.
2. Businesses in Japan are categorized in three groups according to their size: small, intermediate, or large. The definition of these categories varies according to numerous factors, thus complicating statistical study when applying the categories to specific businesses.
3. Ministry of Labor, 1987, p. 113.
4. Ibid., p. 83.
5. Bureau of Small and Intermediate Corporations, 1987, p. 43.
6. Ibid., p. 44.
7. The Law Concerning the Prevention of Delayed Payment in Commissional

Contracts defines the subcontractor as a private or corporate business whose capital is 100 million yen or less and which is in a commissional relationship with another business corporation whose capital is more than 100 million yen. This law was promulgated in 1956.

8. The importance of the rule of mediator in Japanese human relationships is discussed later in "The Horizontal Principle."

9. This Law is discussed above in footnote 7.

10. Kamei, 1985, p. 395.

11. This non-profit association functions to implement various policies for smaller businesses. For the exchange of information and technology in an effort to unify different businesses, the Association has established a subdivision called TICC. It has four major tasks: (1) the dissemination of advice by management and technology experts; (2) the provision of information and technology on production and advanced techniques, in order to meet the needs of individual businesses using light disks; (3) the exhibition of merchandise, panels, and catalogues; and (4) lectures and discussions with experts in management and technology. TICC's motto is "We send accurate messages to ambitious smaller businesses."

12. Some anthropologists, including Toshinao Yoneyama (1976) and Noburhiro Nagashima (1977) have suggested other forms of social organization in traditional Japan.

13. Nakane, 1970, p. 44.

14. Ibid., Preface.

15. Dore, 1958, p. 158.

16. Ibid., p. 159.

17. As one who has often stood between Japanese and American friends, I have hesitated to act as a mediator, because Americans hardly recognize the importance and meaning of mediatorship and how to respond within such a situation, and because I am aware that Japanese rarely tolerate violations of the proper behavior in such situations, even by foreigners.

18. Gekkan Chu Sho Kigyo, November, 1987, pp. 56–8.

19. Ibid., pp. 56–7.

20. Ibid.

4

Passive Individualism among the Youth

Outlook

The impact of individualism from the periphery on the main-stream will be maximized when the new generation becomes individualistic. The attempt to negate feudalistic elements through the promotion of individualism itself is a frequent and universal theme in modernity. It was expected that the emergence of New Men *(shin jinrui)* would have created more interactions between the main-stream and the periphery of the Japanese economy. Although many on the periphery, and even some in the mainstream, who were critical of Japanese groupism found the individualism of the youth invigorating, in the mainstream in general, with its lack of perspective regarding social change, there was fear and worry, doubt about the ability of the New Men generation to sustain the modern culture of technology. Elders in the mainstream were critical of the energetic but restless and impatient nature of the youth, and the passivity they displayed towards social accomplishment was especially worrisome. Those in the mainstream tried to overcome these tendencies in the youth by imposing established values, especially groupism and the work ethic, even more strictly.

New Men

From 1968 to 1987, the popular concept *shin jinrui* spread in Japan like wild fire. The words literally mean "new humankind," with a connotation of "mutants." The term did not have a negative connotation when it first emerged in 1985. The mass media anticipated a positive social change under the initiative of a new generation—a change from the mass production of the age of high economic growth (1955–74) to production of greater variety and smaller quantities. For example, the fashion industry went through a stage of mass production in the sixties, but for the last ten to fifteen years it has flourished by producing in smaller quantities a greater variety of designs. The boom in name brand (usually referred to as Designer's Character brands in Japan) merchandise typifies this new trend, where each fashion product reflects a unique aspect of the designer's character.

Catching up with the fashion industry, the high-tech industry has anxiously changed its direction from mass-production to limited production with great variety. The change in direction has created expectations of high performance from the New Men, and those in the mainstream actively involved in searching for new technological breakthroughs expected that a great many of such creative solutions would come from the New Men. According to Hisashi Shinto,[1] president of the National Telephone and Telgraphic Company of Japan, software production is still old-fashioned and extremely costly. He believes that cost-cutting methods in production as well as less expensive, simpler ways of combining hardware and software must be found. He emphasizes that the talent to make such discoveries cannot be mass-produced.

Yoshitoki Chino, chairman of the Board of Trustees of Daiwa Security, says that the new age demands a new logic and possesses a new language, the artificial intelligence of computers.[2] New Men, he claims, should have minds that are flexible and adjustable. The future of Japan depends on them. Similarly, individualistic owners of high-tech and fashion companies, who are aware of the importance of production in small quantity and great variety, indicated high expectations from the New Men.

Mayumi Yoshinari proudly advocated her faith in the new generation, using a biological analogy:

> Transposon is a gene which constantly changes its position inside DNA. It has insertion places on both ends, and can be disposed in many places in DNA. The

transposon, which is called a "jumping gene" in English, influences other genes around itself without changing its own nucleotide. It is commonly observed in the DNA of lower lives which adjust themselves to the given environment, taking advantage of the mechanism of mutation.[3]

She continued:

Although Molecular Biology has not fully discovered the mechanism of this transposon, I have used it in the title of my book because its free movement, indicating its meaningless-ness in itself, overlaps with my image of today's youth.

The youth today are highly mobile, curious of everything to a certain extent, creating networks of their own and greatly influencing the people around them, but remain noncommittal and are not restricted in their movement. To keep high mobility, they are not possessive. However, they are sensitive to the information about where and how they can receive proper services, and they are willing to pay for them.[4]

Yoshinari is illustrating with her analogy to the transposon gene a category that brings deviant elements into the homogeneous structure of Japanese groups. Usually, joining an established and closed Japanese group requires conversion to its group ethos. Yoshinari has encouraged the youth to join an established group without committing themselves, to leave the group whenever they feel it is advantageous to do so. Her work has added a new dimension to individualism among the Japanese, that is, individualism within mainstream groups. Traditionally, Japanese individualism had been a social option allowing deviants to live in a cultural vacuum. Eshum Hamaguchi's definition of individualism (referred to in chapter 1) in the mainstream of the modern culture of technology characterizes it completely negatively. Yet in 1985, Yoshinari advocated individualism as a new and positive value within the group. To the faithful followers of groupism in the modern culture of technology, her conceptualization was revolutionary.

Failure

Unfortunately, the individualistic movement among the youth, as a generational change, must be seen as having collapsed. Yoshinari's theory of individualism within the group was not practiced by the majority of the youth. Although statistics show a general increase in the number of people who changed occupations in the few years before 1988,[5] this high mobility among the youth is not new, as it has been consistently observed for the last twenty years.[6] Moreover, most settle down before they reach their thirties, preferring the security and prestige provided by lifetime employment in the mainstream. Those who don't enter the mainstream will remain marginal in the society. In their choices, both categories of the youth are simply repeating the traditional pattern.[7]

The notion of the establishment of an independent self, another element in Yoshinari's conceptualization, also held the attention of the upholders of the modern culture of technology. Yoshinari, instead of counseling submission to the given group ethos, encouraged the youth to build independent self-identity. However, the youth, who have adjusted themselves to a given environment for only a limited time without commitment, have not so far had the opportunity to create independent selves. Yoshinari has recommended a negation or a graduation from the "transposon" state, as an independent self can grow only from involvement, confrontation with others, and with oneself. By avoiding confrontation and refusing commitment to any given situation, the "transposon" individuals will not create strong *affective* selves, capable of influencing others and being unaffected by them.

Put-Down

In 1986 and late 1987, more negative characteristics of the New Men were pointed out. They were seen as situational, reactive instead of responsive and responsible, noncommittal, easily hurt, sensitive, and withdrawn. They did not exemplify the "transposons" in Yoshinari's sense—powerful, dynamic, and influential. As the youth's weaknesses became more apparent, the conservative opinion leaders of the economic culture began to criticize them more harshly. Their main concern was the difficulty New Men might have in maintaining the high standard of labor that is the basis of the development of mass production—upon which the modern culture of technology of Japan has been constructed. The words "New Men" took on a negative connotation.

The criticisms directed at the New Men reveal some inconsistencies in the thinking of the opinion leaders themselves. For one thing, the relativistic sense of values held by New Men, pointed out by many as most symptomatic of their corruption, is actually not new in Japanese society. On the contrary, in a traditionally Buddhist society such as Japan, the basic religious value is transientness, and relativism is orthodox. A popular Buddhist saying holds that "Everything which has a form loses it as time passes, and nothing remains constant." Nothing is absolute. There is no legitimate reason for the youth to be criticized for their relativistic sense of values in terms of breaking with traditional Japanese society.

In the criticism against the youth, their relativism is always associated with the work ethic, and implicit in such criticism is the elevation of the work ethic to a value that is inherently Japanese, an indispensable element of the synchronic structure of Japanese society. A problem arises when the youth appear to be unwilling to internalize the work ethic into an absolute value, in the way that older generations have done throughout the process of Japanese modernization. Their unwillingness is a threat to the modern culture of technology.

The following example, taken from a newspaper article, describes a young man who has no attachment to the traditional sense of the work ethic, who has thus "marginalized" himself by having changed jobs frequently:

Takeo Ohara, living in Koenji, Suginam-ku, Tokyo says that he is a free part-time worker. In our old sense, it means that he has no stable job. But when it is interpreted in his way, it actually sounds pretty good.

Until the 20th of this month, he was a part-time cargo worker at the Haneda Airport, Tokyo. After a little rest, on the 23rd, he went to Hachinoki Dake Mountain in the Northern Japan Alps. He found a job for the coming summer in a lodge there. Although his mother in Kyoto is worried and pressures him to find a stable job, he is determined not to. "I am a free part-time worker."

He has had experience in full-time employment. In March last year, he graduated from a top private university in Western Japan. He interviewed with companies wearing a suit called "recruit look," especially designed to give a good impression to the employers.

He liked drawing, so he passed an exam and entered a publishing company doing editorial work for art magazines. In a small office with five or six coworkers, he had all-day desk-work every day.

"I was not fast at manual work," he said. Soon after he started work, someone said to him, "Are you really up to work?" He only remembers today that his body became hot and his head "went crazy."

In May, again someone said to him, "You are not needed here." He listened without saying a word. He did not feel angry. "Maybe I should have." But he felt his body even hotter than the last time.

When he received his 140,000 yen salary for May, he spontaneously said, "I am leaving."

"I did not dislike the work in the publishing company."

"I wish to breathe this freedom I have now. If I had entered a big company, I could have become completely different. I don't know."[8]

After he quit the first job, he went through twenty jobs in approximately nine months. He proudly claims that he is a free man. His kind of overt denial surely frightens those active participants in the Japanese modern culture of technology. His attitude lends credence to their fear that the youth are no longer interested in building identity through group relationships with others. Looking for freedom, even at the cost of security, is a universal characteristic of youth. The conservative elders today fear that the young Japanese many leave their employment positions without having learned how to become harmoniously integrated into a given group.

The following comments are typical of the reactions of the elders to the youth:

Hiroshi Yasukawa, responsible for the employment of transferring workers, is critical of the youth today. "I ask every candidate about their reason for changing jobs. But I rarely receive convincing answers. Most reasons are that the former jobs were too hard or that the wages were too low, indicating their impatience."

Supporting his words, the most common reason for changing jobs (if they do) between fifteen- and twenty-four-year-olds is "too hard to endure in terms of time and physical conditions" (21.8%), and the second most frequent reason given is "too low an income" (18.2%), according to the "Basic Research on the Work Structure" published by the Bureau of Statistics in the Prime Minister's Office.

"Without analyzing their own motives, many youth seen to change their jobs purely on impulse." For example, the reason "the present job is not suitable" sounds reasonable on the surface, but actually is the most ambiguous explanation possible given to Mr. Yasukawa.

Mr. Yasukawa says that selling a car and selling even one piece of *tofu* requires the same amount of effort. Yet the youth who quit their jobs because they are simply uninterested are increasing, Mr. Yasukawa insists. . . .⁹

Discontent

In fact the youth do not radically reject the work ethic itself, but there has been a loss of the sense of corporate loyalty among them. They no longer work enthusiastically, but they still fulfill their given roles sufficiently. Yet because of their manifested value relativism and apparent rejection of the work ethic (merely fulfilling given roles is not enough for the elders of the modern culture of technology), their preference of leisure to work, Japanese youth have been labeled "hedonists." Thus, Tamotsu Sengoku commented:

[The Japanese government] has asked the same questions of the youth of eleven countries every five years beginning in 1973. One of the questions is, "Which is more important in your life, work or leisure?" In answering this question, fewer Japanese prefer work than Americans.

Looking into this data a little more closely, it will be found that between 1978 and 1983 the Japanese youth shifted from preferring work to leisure. In 1978, more than 30% of Japanese youth preferred work, compared to about 24% of Americans. . . . Even the youth were "workaholics" in Japan. However, within five years, the situation was reversed. Now more Americans than Japanese prefer work.¹⁰

In spite of the common assumption of the newness of the New Men, they are not the first generation to be criticized for the loss of the work ethic since the end of World War II. The fact is that the youth, in relation to their elders, have consistently been perceived as threatening. The most distinctive group preceding the New Men was the post-war generation, the youth who were educated under the new democratic system imposed under American guidance. This generation spent their youth during a period of high economic growth, when the modern culture of technology of Japan was in formation. The name given to the antiwork ethic of the youth at that time was "my-home-ism" (*mai homu shugi*). Tadashi Fukutake, a prominent sociologist, analyzed the situation this way:

Now, what consciousness are workers holding in today's Japan in which such a technological reformation stated above is being achieved? According to the

Research on the Consciousness on the Living of Workers done by the Ministry of Labor towards the end of 1971, as far as the degree of satisfaction in living in general both at work and at home, those "well satisfied" number 3% and those "almost satisfied" are 37%; "greatly dissatisfied" count 12% and "slightly dissatisfied" 41%. As a whole, those dissatisfied show much higher percentages than those who are satisfied. The analysis of this research is reported to show that the degree of satisfaction in one's work situation is strongly correlated to the degree of satisfaction in general. In other words, "rewarding jobs" are desired. Those who consider work as either obligation or amusement counted as high as 26% in 1962 according to the research done by National Life Center, but went down below 20% in 1970. And those who coolly separate work and leisure, and who like work but need to rest at the same time, showed gains from 63% to 68%. Besides, looking more precisely into the content, those who consider work to be an obligation greatly decreased, and those who emphasize rest clearly increased. Also, it should be noted that those who wish to stay in a leisurely life are increasing, although their number is still small.

In 1975, according to the research done by the Prime Minister's Office, those who find their satisfaction for living in the family hours count up to 46%, greatly surpassing the 33% who answered that satisfaction came from rewarding work. Generationally speaking, various researches show that the younger or the more highly educated the person is, the more dissatisfied he is with his job, and the harder he tries to find satisfaction in leisure life.[11]

Although Fukutake, as a sociologist, remains objective and analytical in his approach to social change, the shift from the work ethic to an emphasis on leisure became a popular view in the early 1970s. Consumption was encouraged, and the Japanese began to see themselves negating the work ethic on which they had rebuilt their society. Another statistical research on the surface endorses this view: in 1955, 49 percent wanted to work harder than other workers, indicating competitiveness in terms of the work ethic, but 47 percent rejected such an idea; in 1974, the first category was reduced to 28 percent, suggesting 70 percent negated a competitive work ethic.[12] This apparent negation of the work ethic actually indicates a more complex reality: in 1980, 60 percent believed that the Japanese in general were working too hard, although at the same time, only 40 percent of the same group of respondents answered that they themselves were not working too hard. The majority of Japanese believe that they have already negated the affirmation of overwork as a value, whereas others are "behind the times."[13]

The major reason for the complexity of this whole problem is the confusion between the negation of the work ethic and a reduction of corporate loyalty. In 1984, in answer to the question, "Suppose you had enough money to live the rest of your life (without working), would you prefer spending time on leisure or would you still like to have a job?" eighty percent of the respondents, all of whom were company employees, answered that they wanted a job.[14] Besides, 90 percent felt that their present jobs were rewarding, suggesting that Fukutake's emphasis on the importance of having jobs that are rewarding is a concept that is fulfilled even today.[15] This indicates that the work ethic is even more strongly held today than before. One reason contributing to this situation is that physical work conditions in Japan since the early 1980s have undergone marked improvement. The reality is not negation of the work ethic as a social value, but declining corporate loyalty and passivity in work. The Japanese no longer wish to sacrifice themselves for the collective goals offered by their company. The same research shows that two out of three workers believe that fewer of their colleagues in their work situation were ready to sacrifice themselves for their company in the same way that they used to. They also believe that a smaller number now take their work home with them.[16] More extreme cases of declining corporate loyalty have been reported by a wealthy investor whom I interviewed. Some managers of large and established companies in the high-tech industry go to Korea over weekends to sell their professional knowledge to make extra money. To prevent them from doing this, directors of their companies try to catch them at Narita International Airport, before the managers take off on flights to Korea. Although such cases may be small in number, this extreme manifestation on the lack of corporate loyalty is indicative of an undercurrent of rapid social change.

Discontent among younger Japanese concerning imposed corporate loyalty is especially seen in the dissatisfaction with long work hours. Comparative research in 1988 showed that only 35 percent of Japanese from twenty-five to thirty-five years of age are satisfied with their work hours, whereas nearly 80 percent of Americans and British in the same age group answer that they are satisfied.[17] The fact that the majority of younger Japanese want to reduce their work hours undermines the elder generation whose intention is to impose corporate loyalty on the youth, over and against their personal lives.

The conflict between older and younger Japanese is obvious from the following reports: statistics on real work hours (versus work hours entitled) given by the Ministry of Labor (1989) show that the average total work hours in 1988 was 2,111 in Japan and 1,642 in West Germany. The same report indicated that an average Japanese annually works about 500 hours longer than the average German or French worker, and about 200 hours longer than the average American or British worker.[18] Thus, the work ethic continues in reality in spite of a common notion that it is already lost.

Statistics on obligatory work hours (versus real work hours, including hours volunteered by employees) have often misled public opinion, by endorsing superficially the common notion that the work ethic is already lost. In 1985, the national average of obligatory weekly work hours was 41.5 in Japan; 40.5 in America; 40.7 in West Germany; 37.2 in Australia; and 41.8 in England.[19] The Japanese, in comparison, do not appear to be workaholic.

Yet figures compiled by the Central Labor Committee (1987) contradict this impression. In Japanese businesses with 1,000 or more workers, the average of paid and flexible holidays given to workers (in addition to Sundays, Saturdays, and national and company holidays) is 17.9 days. However, the holidays actually taken by workers total only 10.7 days, about 60 percent of the holidays to which workers are officially entitled.[20] These figures show that there is a wide gap between the desires and the reality of workers in Japan. They give up days off when the necessity arises. In this sense, in spite of their discontent, their attitude towards their work situation is still highly ethical.

Privatization of Group

Instead of expressing their frustrations in an active effort to change work conditions, a younger generation has tended to withdraw into small groups. They ignore the larger categories of grouping even that of "Japan." To repeat a point about groupism made in chapter 1, the modern culture of technology is characterized by an overlap of two categories of groups; the first consists of a number of people interacting on a somewhat permanent basis, and the second is a group of people who hold common allegiance to certain ideals or purposes. The first category is limited in membership, because it is established on concrete interactions, whereas the second extends across the nation, because it is ideological and cultural. It was argued in chapter 1 that the aggregation of the group in the first category creates structural pluralism, and that larger grouping in the second category creates cohesion based on the sense of oneness among the Japanese.

The youth's rejection of larger grouping such as that under nationalism actually accentuates pluralism. Instead of submitting totally to already socially established groups, the youth form tight and closed cliques among themselves, or become family men. This tendency represents the privatization of groups. The situation is, on the surface, comparable to America described by Alexis de Tocqueville in the nineteenth century. He noted that:

> The Americans, who mingle so readily in their political assemblies and courts of justice, are wont on the contrary carefully to separate into small distinct circles, in order to indulge by themselves in the enjoyments of private life. Each of them is willing to acknowledge all his fellow-citizens as his equals, but he will only receive a very limited number of them amongst his friends or his guests. This appears to me to be very natural. In proportion as the circle of public society is extended, it may be anticipated that the sphere of private intercourse will be contracted: far from supposing that the members of modern society will ultimately live in common, I am afraid that they may end by forming nothing but small coteries.[21]

Similarly, the youth in today's Japan wish to share their inner feelings among themselves, creating extremely intimate relationships. Americans would probably describe it as a kind of commitment based on an individual basis. But the Japanese do not. The Japanese opinion leaders describe the situation as reflecting a *lack* of commitment, and, again, their assessment is related to the work. The youth are reluctant to submit themselves to the ethos of the company or task groups that were established before they themselves joined. The meaning of the word "commitment" to the opinion leaders is limited to submission to a given work situation, and the youth, they maintain, commit themselves to the wrong groups. In the modern culture of technology in Japan, withdrawal from the task group is equated with withdrawal in general. Identification with alternative groups does not count as commitment.

Reduced corporate loyalty and the privatization of groups may be defined as passive individualism in comparison with active individualism manifested among New Men in such metaphors as *transposon*. While the majority of youth have shifted from active to passive individualism since New Men-ism failed, society, in general, also appears "contaminated" by passive individualism. Withdrawal into family life, in particular, which actually started much earlier, as was pointed out by Fukutake, stands out even more today. By 1983, the breakdown between those who are willing to sacrifice family life for work and those against is 36 percent and 61 percent.[22] Also, in another research done in 1986, 90 percent are contented with their family life, whereas in 1981 only 67 percent were.[23] The most favored private time for today's Japanese is to stay together with their families.[24] Furthermore, 83 percent of the respondents of a research done in 1983 consider that the family is the most essential part of life on which one depends.[25] Endorsing these points made above, the Japanese today hold an extremely positive view of family life. Out of 95 percent who are currently living with their families, 97 percent believe that their family members are all bright and relaxed, and that they understand and trust one another. About 80 percent consider that their households are clean and well-kept, and that the family members observe a high standard of ethical behavior towards each other.[26] As for leisure, 63 percent watch television programs together with all the other members of the family, and 47 percent often go on trips, go shopping and on outings, and eat out together.[27]

This strong attachment to family life is also seen in other statistics about marriage and the relationship with children. Of the respondents over sixteen years old, 62 percent believe that one becomes mature only after marriage, and 90 percent of the married respondents answer that they mutually trust their spouses.[28] The main reason for having children is that it makes work and life rewarding, the second reason is that they like children, the third is that children create a bond for marriage, and the fourth is that it is natural to have children in marriage.[29] These answers already suggest conservatism and the continuing family tradition. Endorsing this situation, the division of labor by sex in the household is accurate: only 4 percent of husbands help regularly with household jobs, although they claim that they are not incapable of doing them. Furthermore, two out of three men and women believe that family life and the household are indispensable for daily life and the socialization of children; more than one out of two consider that the old and the handicapped must be cared for by the family in the household.[30]

Divorce rates and the Japanese attitude towards divorce reflect this situation. Until 1984, the number of divorces and the divorce rate has been increasing, which reached 180,000 cases and 1.50 in 1984, indicating that divorce is no longer socially restricted: moral inhibition has been removed, and women can become economically independent more easily than before. But after 1984 the number of divorces and the rate slightly declined, reflecting increasing changes towards family centrism. Compared to research done in 1977, the attitude of Japanese men concerning divorce has acutely declined, towards conservatism: in every age group the number of those who insist that divorce should be avoided for any reason has increased. The increase among men in their twenties and early thirties who hold this attitude is especially distinctive. Among men today, only those in their late teens and twenties are more positive towards divorce, whereas, among women, the generation below thirty years of age is highly positive. Also, women have shown no great attitudinal change from 1977 to 1984, in contrast to men.[31] These data illustrate a polarization between the majority of Japanese who are attached to an extremely conservative style of household-living and those of a minority who have broken out of this pattern. There is no distinctive group in the middle that is successfully building unique family relationships. In the interviews I conducted, although a few people indicated more possibility of moving in this direction in the future, that is, toward a sharing of household responsibilities between wife and husband, individualism in Japan is not actively practiced within households in the same way, for example, as it occurred in the counterculture movement in America. In today's Japan, active individualism involving daring experimentation is limited to business, whereas a passive form of individualism has been realized partly in family life.

In a sense, this passive individualism, in the form of withdrawal into family life, is a backfiring of the corporate ideology that promotes the company as a family. As Akio Morita, the chairman of Sony, emphasizes, a Japanese economy is solid and efficient when it is considered a quasi-family. Members of the company are well-integrated as indispensable parts of the whole, based on their given role, in the same way that they become part of the kinship relations that define which roles they are to play. Thus, loyalty to the whole and the work ethic that insures the promotion of individual members through the promotion of the whole company derive from this basic structure. Because the members are so well-integrated into the whole, the corporate culture permeates every layer of their social and emotional life. The relationship with the company sets the frame of the mind of each member. The behavior of the company men and women becomes representational of the company epistemology or their shared ethos, in which they take pride and reward. It is a feeling much deeper than simple job-related satisfaction, one that derives from a conviction that one's company is a family.

A problem arises as modern and democratic Japan promotes scientism as a popular social philosophy. The Japanese today apparently have begun to question corporate ideology. The average contemporary number of individuals in a family is slightly less than four, endorsing this observation. Although the pronounced ideal form of the household contains three generations, with three children in the youngest generation,[32] indicating the Japanese attachment to a large household, which may be like a company, in reality today the Japanese are following the practice of forming nuclear families, especially when the wife is younger than twenty-four years of age and, in general, prefers not to have her parents-in-law living in the same household. Obviously, the nuclear family is much more biologically based than the traditional household developed in the northern part of Japan, which became a model for the Japanese-style company. The company may promote a family-like cohesion, but it is still essentially a corporate structure, not a real family. The more the company promotes family-like intimacy, the more its members seek to realize its ideal in their own ways in their private, family lives.

Interaction Ritual

Thus, the patterns of withdrawal into small and private groups become quite understandable, in spite of the claim made by elders that today's youth are totally alien to them. The elders are overwhelmed by the backfire of the corporate family-centrism and the reduced corporate loyalty which is mistaken for the complete demise of the work ethic. A detailed examination of Japanese relationships will explain the strength of Japanese group cohesion, which is quite different from de Tocqueville's American version, and also why the youth cannot transcend collective orientations towards more actively individualistic options and why they become even more closed in their private groups.

Theoretically, human relationships, viewed as a social process, go through three general phases: (1) meeting and developing the relationship, (2) keeping it, and (3) leaving it. The force which pushes a member of society to go through this process is usually a socially shared goal that may be highly ideological in nature. In the case of the Japanese, the goal of a close relationship is perfect mutual understanding, achieved through an interaction similar to what Ervin Goffman conceptualized as "interaction ritual" in North American relationships. Interaction rituals occur throughout all three stages of a relationship, as the persons involved exchange verbal and nonverbal cues. With the Japanese, body movements, tone of voice, degree or avoidance of eye contact, laughter, smiles, serious expressions, and even the degree of body tension are, to a certain extent, carefully controlled to constitute cues.

At the same time, a person tries as much as possible to catch the cues given by others. If a person keeps missing the given cues, he will be judged as "blunt" or "dull" (because he is unreceptive), "impolite" (when it is judged that he is deliberately choosing to miss cues), or *gaijin mitai* (like a foreigner). High receptivity is admired. The Japanese word generally used to indicate such receptivity is *sasshi,* which literally means "to guess." It implies that one guesses the real intention of others in spite of their surface disguise. For example, the Japanese rarely say "no" verbally, but very often indicate "no" in behavioral cues. When the verbal "yes" and the nonverbal "no" are given simultaneously, a good recipient will choose "no" over "yes." He is good at *sasshi* and will be liked. If, instead, the person chooses to hear the "yes," the recipient will likely be able to make the other person do as he has said, but will also probably lose any ties to him in the long run.

Sasshi causes trouble for Westerners, especially for liberal Americans, because they often refuse to label a Japanese hypocritical for saying "yes" and meaning "no." Their trouble is heightened when the Japanese affirm that saying "yes" and acting upon "no" *is* hypocritical. This displays the cultural dichotomy between formality and informality. On a formal occasion, the verbal statement signals a commitment. Deviant actions are prohibited, and actions become impersonal and "formal." In a formal situation, the Japanese adhere to certain principles of behavior, but they are not absolutely fastidious in adhering to them. From the standpoint of principles, of course, saying "yes" and meaning "no" is considered wrong, but in reality and in general (not only for the Japanese), people cannot always stick to principles.[33] The *sasshi* effort to understand this situational restrictiveness is highly appreciated by others.

Although a high *sasshi* ability in the recipient of cues is much appreciated, an expectation of *sasshi* effort from the other is discouraged. The word for this is *amae*. Although *amae* has been co-opted as a psychological concept by Takeo Doi (1973),[34] in the interaction ritual, it is simply used to indicate the restriction of excessive dependency on the *sasshi* of the other person. *Sasshi* is good, but asking for *sasshi* is not; it is considered to be aggressive. *Amae,* when used in a conversation, signifies a passive aggression in which one depends on the manners of the other.

In an ideal and mutually responsive *sasshi* and *amae* relationship, a pair of individuals relate to each other in an atmosphere of spontaneity. Both have mastered how the other upholds and deviates from certain principles of behavior and can recognize when the other is abandoning specific behavioral norms. In such terms, each individual understands the other's consistent patterns in personality. This knowledge and recognition provides a solid basis for mutual trust and loyalty. Each person "masters" the knowledge of the other's personality, thus creating a kind of existential basis for the relationship, a confidence about the other's behavior that serves to ensure that the other will not deviate from the expected behavior.

In this way, Japanese businessmen often appreciate more highly the personalities of people involved in a company than the value of the merchandise offered by the company. Although this is not unique to Japan, the Japanese often consider it to be so and convince others that this is the case. It is not always possible, even for the Japanese, to completely guess the exact meaning of the vague signs of an interlocutor and respond correctly with another set of behavioral cues. Even among the Japanese, when a relationship is distant, as opposed to friendly or intimate, their attitude is formal, reserved, and principle-oriented, avoiding as much interaction as possible. Such behavior serves as a way to avoid confrontations.[35]

As common ground becomes established between two people, the interaction ritual grows increasingly idiosyncratic. At this more intimate stage, the self-expression of each person is facilitated by the articulations and restrictions of *sasshi* and *amae*. An equilibrium in the relationship is established, and it is not permissible, according to the principles of the interaction, to behave in a way that would disrupt it. Even minor changes in ways of relating to each other are difficult to achieve. Such patterns of interaction relate to the particular Japanese sensitivity to constraints in relationships.

A Japanese Game

Based on the give-and-take of *sasshi* and *amae*, the Japanese play a complicated game in developing and maintaining relationships with others. It is so complex and delicate that Japanese tend to assume that it is impossible for foreigners to assimilate it. The following is a quotation from a Japanese book, *Why Is Your Boss Slow to Understand You?*

> There is a type of man who always keeps a stand-off attitude and distance from others. This type of man reminds me of a film entitled, "Whenever We Meet, We Are Strangers."

He smiles and speaks nicely, but is distant and does not try to become close to anyone. He has acquaintances but only a few friends, because he does not expose his real self. To his boss, he is polite and respectful, but is also distant and reserved. When he has a difficulty and when his boss is willing to help him, he only says, "I'm OK," and does not open himself. He refuses to be dependent on his boss. Although it may not sound right to suggest that he should be more dependent on his boss, in fact, in Japan, the boss likes to take close care of his men. Suppose his man brought a problem to his boss, by saying, "Oh, I have a real difficulty. I don't know what to do." The boss will make an effort to deal with it for his man, although the boss may pretend on the surface that he is annoyed.

In exchange, the boss likes to display his power over his man. The boss says, "Can't you do as I say?" and forces his man to obey his order, even knowing that he is abusing his superior position. His man, when he knows what to do, pretends to resist the given order, but says, "Well, I cannot keep going against you, Director." He pretends he is annoyed.

The boss likes to use his power both for helping and controlling his men. Mutual dependency between the boss and his men is a good and comfortable relationship for both of them.[36]

As the above illustrates, the game creates an extremely intimate relationship that is difficult for others to breach. In the modern culture of technology, this informal and intimate relationship overlaps with the formal social organization. It explains why commerce in Japan is perceived as being "closed" and its market as being difficult to penetrate. This kind of closed network of numerous relationships is a functional aspect of social organization in large corporations. In smaller companies, such as family-owned factories that have been integrated into the economic culture, intimate human relationships are even more idealized, since such firms are much more traditional in their values, despite the fact that they may not be able to successfully provide security in the same way as the establishment.

The tendency of contemporary Japanese youth to privatize their groups has led to a separation of informal relationships from formal social organizations. Traditionally, because relationships in Japan are interpreted as being permanent, when a work relationship and a personal relationship overlap, a person is perpetually bound to his work situation through the network of his private relationships. This framework has been the moral basis for the system of lifetime employment in the economic culture of Japan. However, as the youth experiment with new types of relationships, they find that they can leave a work group and at the same time maintain their personal group attachments. At the least, they do not feel guilty about leaving an employment situation and becoming "transposons."

Contemporary Japanese youth has been accused of being "masked," of not revealing their true selves, so that in relation to their bosses, they are "strangers, whenever they meet." The elders of the modern culture of technology worry that because the youth are insufficiently trained in the social interaction rituals, they may undermine the very structure of groupism. Yet the exposure of the real self or of real feelings is actually limited to intimate relationships; the uncovering of the self is expected to occur after a mutual dependency has been established between two individuals. Until that point, people are expected to remain formal, to behave only as they are morally and situationally bound to do. Despite this qualification, the proponents of groupism speak as if their own actions are not "masked" in any way. Their lack of self-perspective reveals just how frustrated the elder generation is by the actions of the youth.

The particular balance of formality and informality is well-expressed in the dichotomy between *honné* and *tatemaé*. In simplistic terms, *honné* is what a person really wants to do, and *tatemaé* is his submission to moral obligation. Interaction rituals begin with mutual expressions that are culturally prescribed when two parties meet; they develop from occasional (i.e., formal) to frequent (i.e., intimate) exposure of honest feelings. The particularities of the moral basis of interaction rituals is socially established and agreed upon. Honest feelings, however, are, by definition, personal. Premature expression of honest expectations can incite a strongly negative response from the other person in the relationship. The Japanese relationship develops very slowly in the beginning, each participant carefully avoiding hurting the other; even a slight offense before common ground is established can drive a person away forever. In the beginning stages, the Japanese may appear extremely reluctant to enter a new relationship. Especially for two persons from different social backgrounds, a tremendous effort is initially required, until a second stage of mutual understanding is reached. After this difficult first stage, when common ground has been established, relationships are sustained by mutual expressions of honesty, played out through *sasshi* and *amae*. Today's youths are problematic not because they do not expose their honest feelings to their superiors but that their expressions themselves are atypical. They are reluctant to enter into the traditionally crucial interaction rituals. By rejecting custom, they ignore the socially established methods that make it easier to overcome initial difficulties and accelerate the slow beginnings of a developing relationship.

Refusal of Social Participation

The insensitivity of the youth is apparent in their attitude toward learning the ritual of social drinking. In Japan, drinking provides a newly introduced pair of individuals with a socially appropriate occasion on which to build intimacy. A British anthropologist once told me that when two Englishmen know they are going to meet as strangers outside of their own homes, they first investigate each other as fully as possible in order to avoid embarrassments at their first encounter. In Japan, two strangers, when introduced, go and drink together as a means of investigating one another. Using alcohol as an excuse, they become outspoken about themselves, ask questions of each other, and, in general, deviate, from normal etiquette, by "exposing their bare selves." This is called *hadaka no tsukiai*, or "having a naked relationship without formality or social ornamentation." In doing this, the two people have entered into an extremely informal situation; an important social rule is that such drinking occasions remain separate from all other occasions. The two people involved remember what has transpired during the drinking occasions, but they do not reveal this when they have returned to more formal social settings. The mutual exploration will continue on the next informal occasion, again by drinking together. In this way, the process of building intimacy is accelerated.[37]

The difficulty that the youth has in assimilating this social custom lies in the loss of ideology that relates drinking to interaction rituals. For one thing, American attitudes against excessive drinking have actively been imported to Japan in the last thirty years. Japanese youth may read about the negative aspects of drinking or study them in sociology and psychology classes. Furthermore, because students are so confined in their intensive preparation for college entrance examinations, they do not have much opportunity to learn from their fathers the traditional custom of drinking, as their fathers learned from their grandfathers. After young people achieve entrance to college or university, they do have more spare time, but they spend it making friends among their peers rather than learning from their fathers.

Compounding this situation is the fact that Japanese fathers are often too busy with their work to be home with their families. In spite of their family centrism, their work ethic is still prevalent, and furthermore, according to the continuing division of roles in the household according to sex, it is still the mother's job to spend the most time with the family's children. The average time per day spent by a father in Japan with his children is thirty-six minutes, compared to forty-four minutes in West Germany and fifty-six minutes in America. Of the children in Japan, 37.4 percent claim that they have almost no time with their fathers, compared to 19.5 percent in Germany and 14.7 percent in America making the same claim. Even on holidays, three times as many children in Japan have almost no contact with their fathers as do those in America and West Germany. In Japan, 40.7 percent of the fathers never help their children with homework, in contrast to 15.8 percent in West Germany and 10.8 percent in America.[38]

American students in the class I taught at the International Christian University in Tokyo a few years ago commonly failed to learn the social function of drinking from their Japanese friends on campus. The majority of Japanese students tell them that they drink because alcohol relaxes them but that they refuse to drink to excess as their elders do. Today, it is less common that Japanese university or college students are aware of the social functions of drinking. Yet the same students, after becoming company men, are expected to master the ritual. The apathy of today's youth toward the meaning of this important social institution symbolizes to their elders an inability to succeed in the modern culture of technology.

Education to Blame

Many among the older generation have accused the education system of being responsible for the behavior of Japanese youth. The older generation, educated before the end of World War II, believes that the nationwide involvement in upward mobility via the educational system necessarily makes the youth competitive, individualistic, and anti-groupist. The emergence of the New Men confirmed their worst fears. In spite of a common Western conviction that Japanese education is oriented towards groupism, the Japanese themselves, in general, believe that American-style democratic education has eliminated groupist values from Japanese schools.

The rule-based competition within the educational system complements the seniority system in employment in Japanese society. The group orientation in the lifetime employment structure to a high degree precludes intra-group competition, not only by the requirement of task performance through teamwork but also by moral and psychological means. Competition among employees is restricted even under the contemporary revised employment system, since all workers are "tenured" as soon as they are hired. As such, there is a selective screening process that prospective employees must undergo. The educational system functions as a social ladder that must be scaled to gain entrance to the mainstream. Entrance into the mainstream is determined by an individual's academic achievement, based on a Western-style, rule-oriented competitive system. Graduation from a top university is the first prerequisite. Although under the revised lifetime employment system, a diploma is no longer a guarantee of automatic promotion over others, as it once was, without it entrance to the mainstream is still generally impossible.

In the same way that entry into the mainstream is limited and selective, so is admission into the top universities. The selection process takes place almost exclusively at the time of university entrance. Dropping out of universities before graduation is rare, as is resignation from any social organization in Japan. An inevitable result of this situation is that entrance into high schools that successfully place students in top universities has also become difficult. Similarly, acceptance to a good junior high school is hard, and even good primary schools are becoming increasingly selective. Thus, even small children are forced to compete for entrance into good kindergartens, for the sake of upward mobility. Schools at each level of education are ranked according to their annual records of promoting their students to good schools at the successive level; these records are readily available to the public through the mass media.

The Japanese educational system is a competitive template imprinted upon youth and through which future elites are selected. In other words, the top stratum in the academic hierarchy shifts into business to constitute its top stratum there. The basic rule for achievement is simple: at every level of the system, a student must clear the hurdle of the entrance examination in order to advance to the next level. All teachers are aware of the requirements of the schools at the successively higher levels; they give each student mini-examinations to test academic ability and place the student accordingly at the next level. This method is called *hensachi* or "differentiating indicator." Since school ranking is determined by the number of students accepted by high-ranking schools at the next level, teachers take their work seriously. In fact, teachers usually compete among themselves in trying to push their own students to higher academic levels. The results of their efforts are duly quantified at the end of every academic year.

Entrance examinations are objective and measure amounts of general knowledge and intelligence. The great demand for fair competition within the educational system has produced objectively graded examinations. Ambiguities are so carefully removed that a given question has only one correct answer. Compositions are often judged to be too subjective, the intelligence and talent displayed therein being difficult to grade, so they are rarely given in lower level examinations. The exception to this are certain private schools that pride themselves on their uniqueness. An unfortunate consequence is that composition is rarely taught, since essays are judged to be useless for academic achievement. In contrast, it is easy to measure *amounts* of knowledge; the history and science books become fatter every year, and the youth are spending more and more time memorizing the contents of ever-thicker books.[39]

The constantly administered small tests and quizzes also encourage students to be competitive. It is an impersonal competition, a setup where students work by themselves to memorize textbooks page by page. Their attention to interpersonal relationships is limited as a result of this system, and they tend to avoid complicated relationships, preferring to relate only to a small number of close friends. It is commonly held that any kind of entanglement with others might be both practically and psychologically costly. Time is valuable, since the all-important examinations measure the amount of accomplishment gained within a given time.

The situation creates a vicious cycle. A person withdraws from wide-ranging friendships because he cannot afford to give time to them. By withdrawing from relationships, the person loses the skills to build them. He loses the ability to deal with conflicts with others or to identify problems and their attendant ambiguities. He becomes threatened by potential conflicts and, therefore, avoids situations with possibilities of conflicts. In doing so, he becomes even more withdrawn. This syndrome has caused an understandable rise in the occurrence of anxiety among elders that the youth are becoming withdrawn, egocentric, individualistic, and asocial.

Value Education

The older generation, being overwhelmed by the fear of Americanization (of which the worst manifestation is individualism), commonly overlooks the fact that the educational system is two-sided. They are convinced that the contemporary educational system, based on American democratic principles and values, totally represses the values of groupism. It is true that those values are not taught as they once were, but they are addressed through the teaching and assimilation of skills related to being a good member of the class. In terms of their importance in upward mobility in the educational system, academic and value competitions are equally weighted. Public attention is almost solely concentrated on academic competition and ignores the fact that entrance requirements consist of two aspects: an objective examination given by the school at the next higher level and an evaluative report on the candidate by the school the student presently attends. The main body of the entrance examination is a series of written tests that usually takes several days; some schools also require the candidate to be interviewed. The report filed by a candidate's current school contains both academic and moral evaluations of the student.

The schools perpetuate a separation of ethical from academic education. An academic evaluation is open; often the results of periodical examinations are posted, so that everyone sees the ranking of students within a school. Students are commonly divided into separate classes based on academic ability. In contrast, the value evaluations are withheld and confidential. They are considered more private, even though both evaluations are crucial to the application process for educational advancement.

The written comments in student school reports carry great weight. A negative comment may be the sole reason for the rejection of a candidate. This aspect of the school report has recently attracted public attention. Nobuto Hosaka, a freelance writer, on 15 July 1988 lost a case regarding his school report before the Supreme Court. His junior high school report had carried the comment that he had been a politically active student. He claimed before the court that he failed to be admitted to schools because of that negative report. The Supreme Court ruled that an objective statement about the student is justified and constitutional and that it does not jeopardize the freedom of speech or belief. Previously, a district court had ruled in Hosaka's favor in 1979, and then a higher court had reversed the decision in 1982. Although this may be an extreme case, it serves to illustrate the importance and enforcement of values in the educational system. Furthermore, public response to Hosaka's case indicates that contemporary attitudes are convinced of the unimportance of value education in the present system and that there was surprise at Hosaka's failure.

Active Passivity

The combination of overtly manifested, rule-oriented competition and the assimilation of latent groupist values in education has led the youth to passive individualism. It is the youth's version of synthesis in the modern culture of technology between individualism in terms of free competition as a Western value and groupism as a Japanese value.

In today's democratic educational system, groupism and inter-action rituals are not taught according to the precise value theory under which older generations studied. It remains latent. The same group value is now expressed by a more general term, *yasashisa,* a noun indicating compassion, tenderness, softness, gentleness, warmth, carefulness, understanding, and non-intrusiveness. Al-though compassion is similar to love in its psychological orienta-tion, their expressions may be different. As has been said, love is expressed as "doing unto others as you would have others do unto you," whereas compassion in the Japanese sense is expressed as not doing unto others what you would not wish others to do unto you. Active kindness, which is an indispensable property of love, does not in itself constitute compassion. Attentiveness to others is seen as being more important, revealing the restrictive nature of the particularism as a value, as has been discussed earlier.

From this basic value orientation, active passivity, an indispen-sable component of Japanese groups, originates. Children in Japan are taught at school to be compassionate, understanding, attentive, and reserved, not pushy or demanding. They learn to listen first and speak second. The difficulty and frustration that Japanese commonly experience in America comes from the fact that their passivity is an *active* expression of their values. To the Japanese, to be quiet and to listen is active, not passive. It is understandably difficult for Americans not to perceive this behavior as a sign of passivity or indifference. In a classroom with American students, students from Japan rarely raise their hands or speak up. They have been trained, as American students have not, to wait for a sign of approval from the teacher. Japanese students may appear polite but unintelligent to Americans. Since active passivity is taken for granted in Japan, it is difficult for the Japanese to understand the American perspective.

Harmony, a standard tenet in Japanese corporations, cannot be maintained without the value *yasashisa,* or active passivity. The members of a group are expected to submit themselves to the group harmony. Even the establishment of harmony should occur harmo-niously; no one should demand it, it should evolve naturally. Once harmony is established, no matter what form or resolution it takes, it cannot be changed by the demands of any individual. Change may evolve in a group, and if it does, it is also accepted harmoniously. As a result, the members of a group tend to be extremely sensitive to one another and tend to be afraid of being left out. Because of the value of groupism, isolation may be interpreted by others as offensive, and those who are perceived to be isolationists may be subject to sanctions. In cases such as this, upholding the values of harmony and passivity becomes a reason to "bully" a nonconformist. This bullying also occurs within the educational system, where nonconformism is a source of annoyance to teachers and boards of education.

The most common pattern of Japanese bullying is the sanctioning of the weakest member of the group by all the others. In spite of the older generation's conviction that today's youth are more individualistic, bullying is still highly evident among them. Such bullying sometimes leads the weakest to commit suicide, which in Japan has the added connotation of being a protest at the cost of one's life, not merely an escape from an unbearable reality. The group, in standing against a deviant, has a chance to display stronger harmony and unity. The group members, with the obvious exception of the sanctioned individuals, experience in the process psychological and moral satisfaction.

It is unfortunate that the outcasts among young Japanese are themselves not free of the group value. An outcast cannot stand up for himself, only partly because he is the weakest of the group, but also because he does not think it is a good thing to do. The adults from whom he may expect help commonly blame the outcast and his attitude, which typically appears disharmonious in their eyes. Such a judgement addresses the result of the outcast's situation, but not the process by which the "disharmonization" of the outcast occurred. The typical recommendation is that the individual should be more actively passive, displaying his harmonious nature and trying to appeal to the compassion of other group members. It would be very rare, indeed, for a teacher to encourage an outcast to stand up and fight against the rest of his group. A teacher who gave such encouragement would himself be in trouble within his own group, the school administration.

The Japanese youth have reacted to these conditions with reasonable tactics: they have formed small, intimate cliques based on trust in one another, as protection. Being recognized as a loner is dangerous. In a large public group a member might become isolated from other members, a loner without recognizing it himself. In an insecure public situation, secure membership in a well-harmonized and privately intimate group is desirable. The student cliques function more as shields against the formal organization than as an integral part of it. The point of emphasis is that the high valuation of passivity actually leads to the withdrawal into small cliques.

Precision

Precision, a major factor in Japanese high-quality production that is promoted through education, actually encourages the youth's withdrawal into small and private groups. The nationwide involvement with academic achievement provides a national consensus on the value of precision, as achieving good results on academic entrance examinations is contingent upon being able to give exact, precise answers. The process of personality development for those involved in upward competition hinges upon the necessity of being precise; it also orients women who wish to become successful and well-appreciated mothers. Those women and men who are not in the competition for themselves are yet in it for their children, trying to develop in their offspring the type of personality that is attuned to precision so that they will succeed.

The word *precision* indicates the elimination of errors and achievement of an exact goal. In Japan, precision standardization, as a positive value, is simply taken for granted. To achieve precision in an issue, product, style, or manner, there must be a given standard. For the sake of precision, the setting and maintenance of standards is beneficient and therefore not to be questioned. According to this rationale, everything in daily Japanese life is given a standard. Most schools up to the high school level have an enforced dress code. It is not uncommon for the length of girls' skirts to be precisely determined by the distance from hemline to floor. Although complaints about such restrictions from liberal mothers appear in letters to newspaper editors, the editorial replies are usually in favor of upholding standards.

One thing that may have been sacrificed for the sake of precision is flexibility. If precision is defined as achieving the standard with little or no error, then flexibility may be defined as keeping the standard optional. I once asked a government official if it were not just as important to be taught how to recover from an error as how not to make an error. He answered that, in the high-tech age, even one error could be fatal. If a mechanic fails to properly maintain an airplane, it could crash; there is no way to recover from such an error. When this same kind of precision is demanded in the game of *sasshi* and *amae,* the number of people involved must necessarily be small; the initial meeting itself becomes increasingly difficult.

Students sacrifice their youth to prepare themselves for a position within the mainstream. Although it may seem a frustrating situation, it also makes the youth appear "romantic," in the sense that they are dedicating the present moment to the potential. As soon as students enter final educational institutions, they try to fulfill their long-standing dreams. A common goal is the development of new friendships. The demand for and high valuation given to precision is expressed as a passive form of individualism which so far fits in the modern culture of technology.

The formation of a passive individualism among the youth has been accepted by the older generations. After an initial period of confusion, the elders have already been successful in integrating the youth into their own system. The active passivity of the youth was easily accessed by employee management forces. The youth will come to work at nine o'clock in the morning, if that is the rule. They will wear company uniforms, if that is the rule, even though they are extremely attached to high fashion. To dissolve any potential conflict, the youth try to somehow coordinate their desires with their work conditions. Young women love to work in boutiques, because there they are expected to be fashionably dressed. As part-time workers in fast-food restaurants, they "act pretty," creating their fantasy world in the work environment. They try to "color" their environment to suit their fancy. Thus, an opinion leader in the modern culture of technology suggests, "Here is a secret to use young help efficiently. By tickling their feelings and likes, management will be well served."[40]

The youth obey the given rules, but they privatize a given situation in order to achieve some personal satisfaction. They may want to revise covert rules built into the modern culture of technology, such as interaction rituals, but rarely do they dare to demand a change in the given framework. A business administrator I interviewed said, "They are only fantasizing about themselves. They are too weak to do anything against us." A sympathizer with the Japanese Communist Party looked disgusted at my question about the New Men's impact on him, saying, "They are annoying. They are so asocial, they cannot form a collective body to initiate a realistic social change." In 1986, such opinions as these were not yet common, but the scorn for New Men intensified in late 1987. By 1989, such opinions were becoming common at all levels of society. Hence, individualism among the Japanese youth is conceived to be passive. It has withdrawn from the public domain of society to privacy, is meekly practiced in the work situation, and is not at all revolutionary in any sense.

However, the same situation indicates that passive individualism creates and accelerates existing structural pluralism against cohesion based on nationalism, thus undermining the ideology of the homogeneous Japanese culture on which the modern culture of technology depends. The strength of passive individualism, practiced as such, is found in its position in the work force in the mainstream. It is not a practice limited to the periphery, but is common among today's Japanese. Although the work ethic does continue, when the structural pluralism is fully expressed in family-centrism, passive individualism will create a momentum for a structural change in the modern culture of technology. For, it will first encourage active individualism in the periphery and, then secondly, it will support pressure from the periphery to the mainstream.

Notes

1. Japan Future Society, 1987, pp. 176–8.
2. Ibid., p. 193.

3. Yoshinari, 1988 (1985), p. 3.
4. Ibid., pp. 4–5.
5. Ministry of Labor, 1988, p. 44, and Statistics Bureau of the Management and Coordination Agency 1988.
6. Ministry of Labor, 1988, p. 44.
7. In the fashion industry, individuals show high mobility, because the field is artistic- and talent-oriented. As well, in some areas of the service industry, people are more mobile, because it is less secure and less prestigious. These particular exceptions do not negate the general tendency.
8. *Yomiuri News*, 2 June 1987 (morning edition).
9. *Tokyo Keizai Weekly*, 1987, p. 23.
10. Sengoku, 1987, pp. 121–2.
11. Fukutake, 1972, pp. 117–8.
12. NHK, p. 54.
13. Ibid., p. 55.
14. Ibid., pp. 69–70.
15. Ibid., pp. 24–5.
16. Ibid., pp. 39–40.
17. *Nippon Economic Journal*, 8 August 1989.
18. Ibid., 16 July 1989.
19. Bureau of General Affairs, 1987, p. 48.
20. Central Labor Committee, 1987, p. 50.
21. Tocqueville, pp. 256–7.
22. NHK, pp. 28–9.
23. Japan Management Association, p. 124.
24. NHK, p. 73.
25. Ibid., pp. 38–9.
26. Ibid., pp. 17–9.
27. Ibid., pp. 19–21.
28. Ibid., p. 57.
29. Ibid., p. 70–1.
30. Ibid., pp. 60–1, p. 34.
31. Ibid., pp. 67–9.
32. Ibid., pp. 15–6.
33. The paragraphs above previously appeared in my "Popularity of Robots in Japan."
34. *Amae* is primarily a neutral word to indicate dependence. However, when it is applied to anyone in a concrete scene, especially through conversation, it indicates excessive dependence and gains a negative connotation. Thus, in a conversation, the word is used to restrict a person from excessive dependence by bringing him to an awareness of his state of being. It can at times be used as a strong accusation, depending on the situation. For example, if a father says to his son, "I am your father," the statement primarily indicates the relationship between the two. However, it may also convey the meaning, "Obey me," depending on the specific context in which that the statement is made.
35. The paragraph above previously appeared in my "Popularity of Robots in Japan."
36. Fukuda, 1977, pp. 20–1.
37. For more information about social drinking, see my "Ritual Men; the Continuing Tradition in Human Relationships Among the Japanese Youth."

38. However, the children who claim that they wish to maintain a good relationship with their father when they grow up number 91% in Japan, 58.6% in America, and 87.1% in West Germany. The traditional ideology of filial piety in Japan continues despite an ideology shift.
39. Attempts to change this situation are being made continually but are mostly unsuccessful. Tokyo University, Japan's most prestigious school, announced that in 1989 it would accept candidates who display unique talents and that this group would be as large as 10% of the incoming freshman class. However, one professor in education, himself a Tokyo University graduate, cynically remarked that the uniqueness recognized by Tokyo University professors, the champions of groupism, cannot be expected to be too unique. The difficulty of setting standards for "unique talents" is a common problem in entrance examinations.
40. Sengoku, 1987.

5

Ritual Men in the Mainstream

Epistemological Closedness

The fact that only a small revision of the rules of interaction on the part of the young has engendered so much fear in the older generation is indicative of the society's heavy reliance on ritual interaction, especially in the male-dominant work situation. This is a major block against active individualism. As discussed, building human relationships upon interaction rituals and the "vertical principle" has given Japanese society both cohesion and, at the same time, variety among groups by creating epistemological closedness and structural pluralism. Although Hamaguchi's analysis does not make clear the "context" of "contextual men"—those who have submitted themselves to the established patterns of interaction rituals within the group—here the "context" seems clearly to be group cohesion based on the framework established through interaction rituals. The framework is particular to a given group and commonly held by the group's members; yet it is not created by the individuals within the group nor is the content of the framework personalized by the group members. It presents itself to individuals as the already established culture of the group. A new member entering a group must submit himself to this group culture. Thus, the opinion leaders of the modern culture of technology insist that the Japanese "self" is situational, a claim usually puzzling to Americans. It simply means that each member has submitted himself to the given framework in the group culture of the work situation. To Westerners, the concept of the situational self carries with it the implication of ego disintegration and associated inconsistency or inauthenticity in the self, and it is viewed as being abnormal or immoral.

The situational self of the contextual men is not, however, characterized by inconsistency. Contextual men actually depend on the consistency that is a quality of the framework of the group. So long as the framework is consistent, the individual self depending on it can maintain consistency. In this way, the individual and the group become harmonious, complementary, and mutually enhancing. This may also serve to explain how emotional security is a well-maintained benefit of the lifetime employment system; the security of a group member is insured by the collective security of the group. Upon entering a group, it may be at first difficult for an individual to engage in the established patterns, interaction rituals, and preset relationships, but the alternative, disengagement and transfer to another set of rules and patterns, would be even more difficult. Such a social structure discourages job shifting. Even for those who do shift employment, their chances to do so are usually limited to only a few times within their lifetime. Furthermore, frequent job shifts make an individual ineligible for employment in the mainstream.

Dependence on Ritual Framework

In order to understand situational or contextual men (or Ritual Men), it is necessary to understand just how the self is dependent on the ritual framework. This major social aspect has been confusingly understood as a result of the ideological shift and adoption of American democracy at the end of World War II. Without further analysis, the theory which ascribed behavior to a set of values belonging to interaction ritual was hastily abandoned as being a component of the war ideology. Furthermore, the adoption of a democratic system and ideals obscured the continuing traditional human relationships insured by the preserved interaction ritual, as it was originally criticized by Chie Nakane. Her theory of "vertical principle" was intended to clarify a partial failure in the adoption of American democracy, not to build a modern culture by validating such a principle which was later considered unique to Japan. Her initial emphasis is placed on the separation between American thought expressed in the formal, democratic, social system and the traditional, Japanese vertical relationships expressed informally overlapping with the former. Today, as a result of this gap, the meaning and the method of interaction ritual are no longer taught together. Confusion between values and group dynamics has become common. The situation has prompted the frustrations of the elders of the modern culture of technology in Japan. They feel compelled to enforce through practice essential Japanese values and interaction rituals, and often accuse the present education system of being too American or of alienating the Japanese from their tradition and for making the youth too individualistic, as discussed in chapter 4.

To explain how the self does depend on the ritual framework,[1] a religious organization used in my fieldwork is a useful illustration, preferable to examining a secular organization, because the former articulates the social context of the Ritual Men much more clearly than the latter. In general, religious organizations elaborate on the doctrine which does teach both the meaning and method of ritual without confusing values with group dynamics, even by denying democratic values. As a result, they are usually considered irrational and socially marginal, and attract criticism from the mainstream. A secular group, in contrast, promotes democracy and scientism, thus making the belief that guides behavior in interaction ritual tacit.[2]

Sekai Mahikari Bunmei Kyodan (SMBK, World True Light Civilization) presents a model case. It is a revivalist religious movement holding an explicit doctrine that directs actions and justifies them. Although the SMBK doctrine has its own special terms, it does, in fact, articulate the meaning of actions by revealing the structure of the epistemological closedness of ritual interaction much better than do secular groups, such as business corporations. As a revivalist movement, SMBK bases its group orientation on an image of order in the universe and a purification ritual. Although its active involvement with faith healing and exorcism separates it from the majority of Japanese groups, the SMBK shows a remarkable affinity with other secular groups in its group formation, especially in its creation of epistemological closedness. In Japanese religious organizations, newcomers must submit themselves to a given set of values, in the same way as new members of a company submit to the corporate culture. Examining how the self depends on the framework established through the purification ritual of the SMBK will give a clear view of how the self in secular organizations is dependent on the framework of interaction rituals.

The SMBK's ritual, in brief, is practiced as follows: its goal, engagement in the perfection or wholeness of the divine universe, is achieved through ritual means. In practice, performers who have not yet been exposed to the doctrine act *as if* they already know the meaning of their ritual actions. The formalized actions of the ritual facilitate this process; formalization separates the form from the content. Consequently, the form in each scene of the ritual is independently perceivable.

Behavioral submission to the SMBK ritual entails a disengagement from the secular way of thinking and assimilation of the SMBK view of cosmological order. Assimilating this order is possible only through behavioral submission, since the new order does not relate at all to any non-SMBK ways of thinking. Without behaviorally adopting the new order through, for example, reading SMBK literature, the new order will make sense only as an extension of non-SMBK ways of thought, through a process of rationalization. In adopting the SMBK order without behaviorally assimilating it, one screens the logic of the new order through a previous order of logic; there is no change in basic epistemology. In the SMBK ritual, on the contrary, the process of simulation through the old logical processes is deliberately blocked. Performers first see the wholeness of the new order in fragments (which, by definition, does not make sense) through the lens of the old way of thinking. Subsequently, a new perspective must be construed, through which all the fragments become intelligible. This perspective is the SMBK order, and it is implicitly offered through the context of the ritual. Thus, ritual enables an absolute change of an individual's epistemological orientation. This process of "conversion" is strictly bound within the ritual framework. Modern society considers this process "irrational," since the change to a new order is achieved without the "approval" of the old order of thought. In a Japanese company, freshmen are forced to go through a similar process of conversion by submitting themselves to the framework contained in the given corporate culture.

When the initiate performer of the ritual acts according to the SMBK logic that he has not yet assimilated, he experiences a separation of body and mind. Through the ritual, a schizoid condition is artificially created. This separation often causes absentmindedness in daily life; the novice performers may become disorganized and confused, forget about time, mistake the day of the week, miss appointments, or be unable to recall their mistakes. Some become so anxious about their ambiguous situation that they become totally self-involved or neurotic. As a counter-solution to such possible consequences, the SMBK simply encourages the initiates to advance to the next stage of initiation as quickly as possible. In a work situation, the change may not be enforced as drastically as in SMBK. However, newly joined members commonly manifest that they must behave *like* company men in the work situation. In the interviews I conducted, they commonly used the Japanese expression, *"Shikata ga nai,"* meaning, "it cannot be helped," indicating their submission to a separation between the given and their natural state. They say that, in the work situation, they are supposed to act out an image as company men that they have not yet assimilated.

The "twilight" state of separation of mind and body may be avoided by an initiate remaining at the lowest level of dedication to the SMBK; participating only once in the ritual as a passive performer does not require willful commitment to the SMBK order. However, after the initiation, acting as an active performer requires a firm commitment to the SMBK belief system, a belief in possession by spirits. Without this belief, it is difficult to speak to the possessing spirit as having a real existence rather than as an aberrant psychological manifestation. Since the idea of communicating with a spirit has no basis in secular thought, the advanced SMBK ways of communication such as "investigation" (identification of the possessing spirit) and "admonition" (teaching of the doctrine) are considered impossible without a real commitment to the SMBK order. In the work situation, the initial submission to the given somehow must change to a more active commitment, in order to behave more naturally as a part of the whole of the company. In the attempt to engage or commit oneself, as a condition for advancement to higher levels, one must experience this "twilight" state. Victor Turner (1969) lists various conditions as being properties of *liminality*. Such conditions may also apply to the artificial creation of a process of disengagement from an old logic toward engagement with a new cosmology.

Within the established ritual framework, SMBK believers above the advanced level (senior believers) are more relaxed and have achieved more flexibility than others; they are more spontaneous. The ability to be spontaneous is required for such advanced ritual acts as admonition and investigation, the focus of spirit communication. The possessing spirit is not made to leave against its will but rather is persuaded to leave of its own accord. If a possessing spirit is forced to leave, it is believed that it must go straight to Hell. The SMBK does not permit engagement in such excessive uses of power—even over evil spirits. The purpose is to "heal the spirit" of both the possessor and the possessed. For this purpose, admonition is particularly important because the possessing spirit must be convinced to leave. Prior to admonition, investigation is necessary. To the SMBK, sin is not a general state but a particular mistake one has made. It has to be precisely identified, and all persons involved in the situation must be identified. Thus, admonition is not a simple preaching of general moral principles; it leads to the unfolding of a long story about how the mistake was made and how it has influenced others. The efficiency of the exorcism and the accuracy of the unfolding story depend upon the skill of the ritual performer, measured in turn by his degree of spontaneity.

In secular groups such as business corporations, there is no investigation or admonition of spirits. However, the interaction rituals of a group have their own levels of mastery. Senior members who have mastered the group ritual display spontaneity. Their actions, state of mind, and emotions are all well-synchronized and demonstrate superior faith in the group. Compared to the senior members, those who have newly joined a group exhibit a high degree of awkwardness. It is easy for the masters of the ritual to "see" from the actions of the newer members their level of assimilation into the group. In ritual, the degree of loyalty to the group becomes *visualized* in individual behavior, providing members with a firm ground upon which to act, think, and feel, within the boundaries of the ritual framework. Since such "visibility" depends on participation within the framework of the group, those outside the group will be unable to "read" the behavior exhibited by an insider. Thus, this epistemological closedness becomes a particular component of the Japanese group and, accordingly, of structural pluralism.

Under these conditions, if the youth become able to change their group affiliations freely based on their will like "transposons," to achieve independent selves, they have achieved a great accomplishment. Today's youth, however, should be called Ritual Men instead of New Men, since the majority have not, in fact, moved away from traditional group orientation, and, consequently, remain a high-quality labor force because of their dependency on a given framework. The slight modifications that they have made in terms of passive individualism reflect the shift to production in smaller quantity/greater variety, by creating fine differentiations in products. Thus, passive individualism fits well in the context of the current social change associated with the changes in production modes towards even higher technology. Groupism, epistemological closedness, and dependence on the framework of the given corporate culture are all considered positive values in support of the work ethic.

Cross-Cultural Relationships

The domestic benefits of groupism, in any form, however, have proven to be a hindrance in international business. A person who has behaviorally adjusted to a given framework has difficulty in acting spontaneously in different frameworks. Epistemological closedness, within the boundaries of ritual framework, offered to Ritual Men a firm ground upon which to act, think, and feel. Yet this same closedness has blocked them from reaching out and viewing the frameworks of others. The insider-outsider distinction in terms of group membership is not simply a matter of the different values that the distinct categories hold but is highly epistemological. Because their understanding of others depends on being about to "read" behavioral cues and signs in interaction rituals, when they cannot interpret in this way they cannot understand one another.

Understanding among insiders who are conditioned to "read" one another is spontaneous. Yet, for the same reason, perceptibility between the insiders and outsiders of a group is deficient. As I have already discussed, this pluralistic structure in Japanese relationships requires a go-between who bridges the members of different groups. Unaware of this essential problem even in their domestic relationships, the Japanese in most cases do not know how to relate to the larger panorama of worldwide cultural pluralism. The overlap of frameworks in cross-cultural interactions confuses Ritual Men. In this social context, a contemporary separation between the theory and the method of ritual interactions and associated value confusions in secular groups ironically create a momentum for individualism. First, the separation relaxes the behavioral enforcement of the given epistemology. Company ethos may be shared emotionally, but may not precisely ascribe every single action to implicit rules contained in the corporate culture. Second, overcoming confusions necessitates intelligibility beyond a simple reading of behavioral cues and signs. The framework must be objectified and articulated. Through this task, a Ritual Man individuates himself. He stands above the given social system, at least in his understanding, and is no longer encapsulated in the closed epistemological framework. Hence, the ideological shift from the traditional values to postwar democracy provided the Japanese with such conditions as objectivity and individualism for internationalization and economic success, through reorganizing its initial confusions.

Japan's contemporary economy is intertwined with overseas markets, although its foreign trade dependency of about 10 percent is not nearly as much as it has been believed to be. It is, in fact, much smaller than that of other economically active Asian countries. However, the increasingly international responsibility Japan must now take on as a new economic superpower makes it necessary for Japan to initiate dialogues with other nations. In the 1960s, a majority of the Japanese viewed marketing abroad as a simple, mechanical process. Japan merely had to produce merchandise that would sell well in foreign markets. It seemed both logical and practical that merchandise would walk into a new market by itself. However, the Japanese were rapidly forced to realize that marketing and deal-making was not a mechanical but a human process. They were faced with the disturbing fact that consumers held a poor public image of them and were slow to buy products of Japanese origin. They had to realize that markets abroad consisted of people whom they did not know, and that their sales successes depended on understanding the psychology of these unknown people. Overseas markets have been found by contemporary companies, such as Sony,[3] which has invested in the goal of understanding cultural differences. Their personnel are among the few individuals who have endured direct exposure to Western cultures. Such cross-cultural understanding further demands that an individual be able to objectify his own cultural background. In doing so, he becomes "individuated," not in the sense of Hamaguchi, but in Yoshinari's sense. The individual becomes a "transposon" and crosses cultural boundaries.

However, the reality is that the majority of Japanese still are known for withdrawing into small groups for protection when outside of Japan in the same way that the Japanese youth take refuge in private groups. This way of adjusting to foreign cultures has become more common as more Japanese tend to temporarily settle abroad for business reasons. The alternative is "conversion" to the new framework into which an individual has been thrown. It is a total replacement of the social template of "Japaneseness" or groupism with "non-Japaneseness" or individualism. The business leaders who remain in Japan frequently lose capable field personnel through this kind of conversion. They attempt to reinforce the field employee's sense of his own Japaneseness and the corporate faith more strongly. But this compensatory action often backfires by making the field employee even more strongly attracted to change.

Trying not to be Re-integrated

The problem is regularly observed among so-called returnee students,[4] those youths who have been living abroad with their parents and then return with them to Japan.

Typically, they have been placed in local schools while abroad. They must submit themselves to the local set of values in order to be "good students." It is difficult for such students not to want to excel, due, in part, to the fact that their parents, usually having been sent abroad by their corporate employers, are elitists who want their children to be academically successful. The young students, trained in Japan to meld with a group, naturally feel obligated to adjust themselves to the ethos of local groups where they have been transferred. Consequently, they end up converting to local values, frequently contrary to Japanese-style groupism. The Ministry of Education has mounted a major campaign to re-integrate returnees. Once the Japanese way has been abandoned, reeducation is difficult to achieve. As a result of the inability of many Japanese to deal with this phenomenon, most returnee students find themselves socially shunned. Increasingly, however, returnees, with their acquired language skills, are being recognized as a valuable resource in Japan's efforts towards further internationalization—provided they can return to functioning successfully within Japanese groups.

Under these social changes, an interesting and new alternative in education for such returnees and nonconformists is available at international schools. These schools, built initially for the education of non-Japanese students, provide an educational alternative outside groupism. The number of such schools is still as small as thirty. But they have attracted attention from parents who want to keep their children from being integrated into the mainstream values and, as a result, have attracted negative pressure from the Japanese government that promotes nationalism and discourages diversity in Japanese society.

Below the college level, such schools are more or less like American schools built to educate American children living outside of America. In major cities in Japan, there are many non-Japanese children of different nationalities whose parents are working there. The majority go to international schools where the education is mainly given in English (and some other European languages). Japanese is treated as a second language.

Besides such non-Japanese visiting students, international schools have also attracted the children of wealthy Asians, such as

Koreans and Chinese, who have settled in Japan. The parents may be unable or reluctant to become Japanese citizens, and they anticipate that their children will be marginal in Japanese society because of their non-citizenship. Such parents have accepted their non-elitist position in Japanese society; although wealthy, they do not have prestige.

Following the example of these Asians, some Japanese who stand firmly as non-elitists, whether or not they themselves are part of the formative new elitism, send their children to international schools in order to avoid the restrictive education dictated by the Ministry of Education. Parents who have achieved success in the business world, without having succeeded in the Japanese academic system, believe that the academic training under the Ministry system is not essential to their children's success. They are frustrated by the governmental educational system that remains monolinguistic and monocultural. They prefer their children to have a bilingual education, an essential qualification for succeeding in international business. Although international schools do not teach Japanese as intensively as their counterparts, the Japanese parents of children in the international schools assume that by virtue of the fact that they are living in Japan and that Japanese is spoken in the home, the children will be fluent in Japanese as well as in English.

The Ministry of Education and the local Boards of Education are highly critical of and strongly opposed to this movement among some Japanese parents. According to their definition, the international schools are not Japanese schools for Japanese children. Most of them have not been given approved status, and their standing remains similar to a cooking school or a private company whose business is education. Their diplomas are not valid in Japanese society. If Japanese students of international schools wish to advance in Japanese universities or to transfer to regular Japanese schools, they must take qualifying examinations in Japanese, given annually by the Ministry of Education, or obtain the status of returnee student, through negotiation with the Ministry. Alternatively, they go abroad for two years and return as official returnees.

In general, the Ministry of Education and the local Boards of Education hold that it is not desirable for Japanese children to be educated like foreigners. A Japanese mother whom I interviewed told me the following story. Since she divorced a few years ago, she had been working for an American high-tech company as the secretary to the president. Because she wanted her nine-year-old son to be "international," she decided to send him to an international school where he has been educated in English. Soon after he entered the school, she received a call from a member of the local Board of Education, saying that she was neglecting the legal obligation to educate her Japanese children to become Japanese. She could not understand this, since the international school she chose was neither American nationalist nor religious. Also, although she spoke English well herself, her own identity was strictly Japanese and she was unconvinced that an education in English for her son would de-Japanize him.

She was also questioned at the Taxation Office. When she filed her tax return, the officer did not believe that a single woman could receive such a high salary, sufficient for her to be able to afford to send her son to an international school, whose tuition is high. Finally, she decided to send him to a boarding school in America. At the time, the American Embassy was not pleased, assuming that she was sending him there so that she could follow him to immigrate to the United States. She is not a rare exception under today's intensive internationalization. More and more women are becoming economically well-off enough to experiment with different life-styles. Women today face choices between marriage and work that often appear to be mutually exclusive. Although the majority still choose the safe and traditional solution, some decide to choose economic independence. Among them, there is a polarization similar to that of men. Some of them try to join the establishment, in the same way that men do, and others individuate themselves and become more experimental, both types want the same rights as men have.

Tamie Nojima (pseudonym), another career woman I interviewed, was raised in England and educated primarily in English because her father had been sent abroad to work for his Japanese company. Although her fluency in foreign languages is a definite advantage in her career, her foreign-bred personality is viewed as a liability by her male Japanese colleagues. However, during the course of our interview, she behaved in a very Japanese manner:

natural, open, a little nervous, and she spoke with no trace of a foreign accent.

Because she is trying to succeed like men in the mainstream, she inevitably encounters more difficulties. She says that she has to shift her attitude completely when dealing with her Japanese male colleagues, in contrast to her relations with her non-Japanese friends. In the presence of her male Japanese colleagues, she behaves as they would expect a Japanese woman to behave, whereas with her non-Japanese friends she feels comfortable being more expressive.

Nojima feels that the Japanese government, as a typical mainstream social organization, is excessively male-dominated. There is usually only a single woman per year who achieves senior diplomatic status, and one such woman's passing of the senior diplomatic examination was recently treated as a newsworthy event in the Japanese press. Nojima also complains that, despite her willingness, she does not have the opportunity to display her abilities, because such behavior would not meet the level of passivity required by the Japanese code. Although such passivity is required of both men and women, men are given chances to actively display their personal abilities, whereas women, according to Nojima, are not given such opportunities. A woman's display of ability without male permission is seen as threatening and offensive. Display of abilities must occur within a given framework, and it is considered rude for a woman to push for such permission.

Confrontation Avoidance

A major part of Nojima's, and other individualists', difficulties arises from an aversion to the practice of confrontation avoidance, essential to the Japanese value system. The creation of an autonomous and dynamic self requires the ability to face contradictions and confrontations. But this attitude is not socially encouraged in Japan as a desirable state of mind. The avoidance of disagreement or conflict does not allow for problem resolution; instead, it perpetuates them. It is a static and defensive position. In contemporary Japanese society, a person such as Nojima often compartmentalizes behavior and attitudes to relate to different situations demanding varying orientations and expressions. In such situations, the ego suffers from lack of spontaneity and integration.

Confrontation avoidance is automatized in Japanese interaction rituals. Two parties must be polite at the beginning of the formation of a relationship; those from different groups are strangers to one another, each with a somewhat different ethos and behavioral patterns. In this context, even fellow Japanese are foreign to one another. For the sake of politeness, the Japanese withdraw quickly and willingly from possible differences with others. Those foreigners who are used to dealing with the Japanese follow the Japanese rules and withdraw from possible contention; with their appreciation of the patterned Japanese politeness, such outsiders are well received by the Japanese. Such self-withholding or "trimming of self-appearance" is socially reinforced. An encounter between an outsider and an insider where such behavior is observed is usually successful, provided that neither exposes anything personal to the other. According to the rules of the game, a way of avoiding the source of confrontation must be found, so that the problem can be deliberately ignored and both individuals agree to consider the problem "gone." An obvious downfall of this system is that a problem that has been ignored may recur with greater impact, thus becoming more difficult to ignore or circumvent.

The stricture of confrontation avoidance forces the Japanese to be manipulative with each other. In a social situation, instead of asking outright what the others might like to do, they "constantly scheme to move each other."[5] When Japanese objectify and manipulate outsiders, they avoid any sense of confrontation. Confrontation occurs only when group members allow themselves to be exposed to the different sets of values held by outsiders. The group member then has to endure the feeling that his own values are being challenged or questioned. In essence, he is confronting his own values through the exposure to different ones. An individual who allows himself the experience of such value confrontations may be said to be "open" to others.

It should be noted that the fear of confrontation is often the cause of confrontation. When one's own values are objectified by exposure to an external reality, an ultimate confrontation takes place. The display of differing attitudes and behavioral patterns by outsiders is often quickly perceived with fear by an individual, who interprets the display as an attack on his own values. Yet to claim that the situation is "unfair" or discomfiting is to create another conflict. In the effort to avoid confrontation, much latent confrontation is actually generated. This is a major reason for the uneasiness toward individuals on the part of Japanese who espouse groupism.

Out of Ritual Context

What follows is an analysis of a failed attempt to create a cross-cultural relationship based on Japanese-style interaction rituals, taking place outside of the Japanese social context.

A Japanese woman in America, young enough to be automatically categorized with the New Men, isolated herself from developing a sense of active individualism or an independent personality. She held on to traditional values, thinking to create a better future for herself. She wanted to master Western languages by studying abroad, and to later use these skills as tools to climb up the career ladder of success. The demand for those with Western language skills is high in the Japanese job market. A common conviction among the Japanese is, "We do not speak foreign languages well because we are confined to Japan; any one of us will be able to learn any language once we are released from such confinement." In reality, however, most Japanese prefer to shield themselves behind their cultural barriers even when abroad. Many Japanese students in America concentrate solely on their intensive language courses, avoiding socializing with American students. Their behavior parallels that of the hard-working students in Japan who are constantly preparing for successive entrance examinations. Both the students in Japan and those who study abroad share a desire for intimate relationships with only a few good friends, based on *sasshi* and *amae*. Japanese students abroad commonly extend this practice, instead of opening themselves up to the possibilities of new kinds of relationships with others.

I interviewed a nineteen-year-old Japanese student who was studying abroad and lived in a college campus dormitory:

Q: Have you made American friends?
A: No. Maybe one . . .
Q: How often do you see him or her?
A: I see her once every few weeks.
Q: Don't you want more friends?
A: Yes.
Q: Do you go to parties? This is the standard way of meeting people here, and it is the first step in making friends.
A: No. I do not like parties. I cannot stand them. I hate to be introduced to many people at once. I do not like the atmosphere.
Q: Then, what would you like to do?
A: I would like to have a few intimate friends [of the same sex], and that's all [I want].
Q: How will you find them?
A: I don't know. . . .

Her case is typical. She wants her friendships to develop in accordance with Japanese values and the associated relationship patterns and does not consider alternative ways of making friends. American methods of establishing relationships are too difficult for her to assimilate.

In Japan, intimate relationships are formed primarily among friends of the same sex, with no sexual connotation. Men, as has been noted earlier, have their own socially correct ways of establishing intimacy, such as the ritualizing drinking occasions. Women's patterns of establishing intimacy are different. The young Japanese woman interviewed above wishes to have safe and intimate friendship with several female friends, avoiding potential entanglement with male friends. To her way of thinking, it would be more straightforward and easier to start learning about a new culture through a small number of intimate friends, and then to expand friendships through them. But she is unable to initiate relationships that would result in such intimacy.

Finding friends is a big step, but keeping them is an even further one. Many students I interviewed were in the process of losing their American friends, without even realizing it. To the Japanese, friendship is intended to be lifelong. In principle, once it has become established, it cannot be dropped. Ending a relationship is highly offensive. Thus, the Japanese develop relationships slowly, keeping a safe distance and an escape route open, allowing either person to drop the process of developing friendship without causing social "damage." At this initial stage, if problems come up, both persons keep their distance and the relationship stops developing. Both individuals may psychologically distance themselves at this point, but the relationship itself is allowed to remain in limbo, never overtly ended. On the other hand, after an initial stage of formality, a new relationship may extend into an informal and personal stage, in which both individuals become intimate and emotionally involved with each other.

For the Japanese who have grown up with this social orientation, adjustment to American ways is difficult. They consider that American relationships develop too quickly and that they are abruptly dropped when one party feels the relationship is too burdensome. To the Japanese, this seems totally unfair. In such a situation, it become impossible to keep a safe emotional distance. What is most shocking to the Japanese is the high turnover rate in Americans' networks of friends. For example, at an American party, everyone tries to add new members to his circle of friends, but by doing so may drop some old friends, as the number of friendships that can be maintained is limited. Americans, in establishing long-term relationships, must keep old friends while also adding new ones. Although contact patterns and ways of maintaining relationships vary among individuals, in America this is the standard process of making and having friends. In this sense, it can be asserted that Americans are culturally homogeneous. The common desire among Americans to improve one's social standing by associating with an increasingly select group indicated a high degree of competition, which, for the Japanese, is what must be avoided.

Japanese students in America, by reacting defensively to the difficulties with which American culture constantly confronts them, neglect the fact that learning a language is contingent upon learning its associated culture. A Japanese student in America, practicing the confrontation avoidance that is a major value of groupism, cannot reach beyond cultural boundaries or understand people who function under different social frameworks. This quandary points to an essential defect in ritualistic orientation itself, that is, the confinement to and reification of the given ritual framework. The questions that here arise are whether there are alternative ways for the Japanese to extend themselves beyond their cultural boundaries and whether the growth of peripheral individualism might provide that way.

Toward Internationalization

I have discussed why the Japanese have difficulties becoming "cosmopolitan." Ritual Men, who depend on a given behavioral and epistemological framework, cannot bridge the gap between themselves and others. The problem surfaces in the cultural confrontations that the Japanese experience abroad, especially when the values of groupism are threatened. It is one of the major problems that receives public attention in Japan today.

However, the issue of cosmopolitanism is only a small part of the process of the internationalization of the Japanese. When the modernization process began, as a shift from traditional values to Westernization, modernization was seen as synonymous with Westernization or internationalization. Although only a small number of Japanese were directly exposed to Western cultures, the remaining Japanese had to adapt to Westernization through the cues and information given to them by those who had experienced the West firsthand. Today, a synthesis between the two sets of values has taken place, and modernization no longer is interpreted as meaning the internationalization of the entire population. The modernization of Japan has also developed through the interactions of its own social components, especially between the dominant groupist culture and the peripheral individualist culture. In other words, an individual now has the option of whether to participate in the further internationalization of Japan.

High-technology scientists and those scientists involved in theoretical work feel most keenly the need to bridge cultures and further the internationalization of Japan. Even in the importation of Western theoretical developments, these scientists are aware of the great cultural gap between themselves and the West. As Ritual Men, the Japanese are accustomed to pay attention to concrete matters of daily life. This has made them prosper in the applied sciences. For this reason, they are less interested in theorization, which seems to them too philosophical and abstract. Instead of expending energy in the exhaustive task of doing their own theoretical research, the Japanese have imported theories from the West. In the modern culture of technology of Japan, Ritual Men develop practical and technological applications from these theories. Consumers are indifferent to the theory behind products. Those scientists who want to further develop Japan's modern culture of technology, to continue to lead technological development in Asia, are aware that theoretical development must be a priority, and they are also aware of the public's attitude of disinterest.

Another group of people who are intuitively aware of the necessity of theoretical development are those business people who are sent abroad and find that their inability to abstract or theorize about their experiences is a handicap, especially since when they are abroad they have specific goals to accomplish. They become remarkably opinionated and argumentative when they attempt to communicate their experiences in an abstract way. Since they cannot abstract from experience, away from the site of exposure they lose the knowledge of the experience. It does not go beyond the here and now. Memory soon becomes distorted and fades. Returning to Japan, they do not often find people who can relate to their experiences or their strange habits of explaining themselves. The inability of Ritual Men to think with a high degree of abstraction makes it difficult for them to stand at the interaction of cultures or even to see their own stance clearly. Their intuitive grasp of theory does not, by itself, lead to further articulation of theory. They do not know how to reach into the realm of the abstract and synchronic, beyond the here and now, the immediate and concrete. They do not perceive a particular object or idea as related to another. Such relationships appear obvious only through the mediation of the process of abstraction. Those who stand at the intersections of cultures who do think abstractly are able to comprehend the essence of other cultures, by varying their own perspective. This process is a form of theorization.

Neither the opinion leaders of the modern culture of technology nor the Japanese government is ignorant of this deficiency in the mainstream culture of Ritual Men. They are looking for ways to encourage the development of theorists in Japan, without losing them to the opportunities they would find in the West. From this vantage point, even the most radical upholders of the modern culture of technology admit that the negation of particularism, the central value system of Ritual Men, is crucial to the future success of Japan, and they agree that individuality is now a necessity. Nonetheless, when a person does exhibit individualistic characteristics, he is still strongly pressured to fit into the existing social context of groupism. Even though the opinion leaders elevate the creations of individualistic innovators, they refuse to give credit to individualists. Obviously, those in the mainstream are caught between the necessity of reproducing Ritual Men to sustain groupism and the increasing demand for individuals who can take the initiative in further internationalization, in its wider sense.

Notes

1. Miyanaga, 1983.
2. I have written about the loss of ideology in postwar secular Japanese society, ideology being that which specifies the meaning of actions. See my "Ritual Man: Continuing Tradition in Human Relationships among the Japanese Youth in Japan."
3. Morita, 1986.
4. White, 1988.
5. Kenelm Burridge, on his visit to Japan in 1985.

Conclusion

In recent Japanese history, the expression of individualism has been marked by a departure from the place it traditionally occupied in Japanese society. A new form of individualism has emerged among entrepreneurs, experimental and small in their organizations, who have taken advantage of the flourishing Japanese economy. It is their business style—risk-taking and independent—that makes them stand on their own and categorizes them as "individualistic." The phenomenon of individualistic entrepreneurs has also been observed in other Asian countries that have undergone the process of modernization. A universal feature of individualism in Asia, distinctively obvious in the example of Japan, is that entrepreneurs, once they have achieved social and economic success, willingly enter the mainstream, instead of striving to retain the individualistic values that helped them achieve that success. Such "conversion" to the mainstream is often characterized by shifts from apolitical stances to close connections with the government, from egalitarianism to a place in the social and economic hierarchy, from affinity for organizational openness to closedness, from heterogeneous group memberships to a more homogeneous social orientation that emphasizes sameness and commonality, and even to upholding the concept of unique corporate ethos that remains incomprehensible to outsiders. Since 1868, throughout the period of Japan's modern history, successful entrepreneurs have successively entered the mainstream's cycle, contributing to the collectivity of Japanese society. The giant manufacturers in the automobile and electrical industries today who commonly started as entrepreneurs shortly after the end of World War II, are also good examples of this trend.

The social balance between the individuation of members of Japanese society and those successful, powerful individualistic members who reintegrate into the mainstream has given a fundamental stability to Japanese society.

This cycle, which has already been established as a tradition in modernity, has recently been interrupted by those more *actively* individualistic entrepreneurs, who are determined to keep their organizations small and non-conforming; they refuse to expand their businesses in size even when they achieve the economic means to do so. The first champions of this phenomenon were the fashion designers of the 1970s, followed by the high-tech designers of the 1980s. They have disseminated individualistic values not only through unique management styles and lifestyles but also through the products of their businesses—which are often external expressions of their personal views and beliefs. Active individualists firmly contend that their individualism is the source of their creativity, and, accordingly, the key to their success.

Yet the majority of the Japanese still view individualism as deviant behavior. A major reason for this is that Japan's economic success, which is still concentrated in the mainstream, has been built upon the foundation of corporate loyalty, imposed through particular forms of collective group orientation. The elders in Japanese society argue that this foundation is essential to Japan's further economic success and technological developments. They assume that economic success is dependent upon the defense of Japanese values, and they refuse to relinquish those values. They believe that the value of groupism is the essence of Japanese culture, consistently existent throughout history, and that every Japanese is born with an innate Japaneseness. Social scientists have argued that groupism forms the synchronic structure of Japanese society and of the Japanese psyche. This view is the opposite of common Western assumptions about modernization and technological development; that is, that the process of modernization in the non-West should involve a shift from non-Western traditions to the adoption of modern Western ones. During the period of its modernization, Japanese society did try to copy the West, and it suffered feelings of inferiority in relation to the West. Then, in the 1970s, the Japanese, still in the process of transition from their own tradition to Westernization, found themselves in the midst of economic prosperity. At first, it was assumed that the Japanese should continue the process of transition, and that Japan's economic prosperity was a result of this Westernization process. Soon after, a shift in perception occurred; the Japanese realized that their economic prosperity was due to the *uniqueness* of Japan as a nation, not as a result of its Western assimilation. Japanese tradition once again became a positive value to its society, and the Japanese turned from further assimilation of Western values to the defense of Japanese ones. Nakane's theory of the vertical principle, originally constructed as a critique of the delayed and incomplete transition to democracy in Japan, was adopted as a guideline for the construction of traditional human relationships in modern Japan, forming the basis of what has been termed the modern culture of technology in Japan.

I have suggested that what is happening in Japan is neither an incomplete shift from traditional values to Western ones; nor is it a defense of one against the other. Rather it represents a synthesis between the two cultures, traditional and Western. This third perspective makes clear the differences between Japanese tradition and Western modernity. At the same time it throws light upon the unique modernity of contemporary Japanese society, a modernity different from that of the West and yet in many ways as successful in its achievements. The transformation of individualism from its traditional peripheral dwelling-place to its now-prominent relation to the modern culture of technology is one of the most illuminating aspects of the way that Japanese society is characterized by a modernity that it can call its own.

As discussed earlier in this book, individualism in Japan was traditionally viewed as a social option for deviant people who did not fit into the mainstream of society. Many people, in order to live their own lives, felt compelled to leave the mainstream culture that so rigidly bound its members. They commonly took refuge in art and religion, some forms of which were much freer and liberating as practiced on the periphery than in the mainstream. In fact, the formation of a silent subculture through the compartmentalization of socially deviant individuals is common in non-Western traditions. Since power, prestige, and economic security are the monopoly of the mainstream, those deviant populations compartmentalized on the periphery are powerless and thus represent no threat to the establishment. In many cases, the separation and juxtaposition of the mainstream and the periphery actually served to strengthen the status quo in the power structure, as individualists were held up as negative exemplars of asocial lifestyles, reminders of what correct lifestyles should be.

In the modern culture of technology in today's Japan, the maintenance of the values of groupism is dependent upon the exclusion of individualists from the mainstream of society. Japanese groups are so rigidly collective that any ill-fitting elements disqualify one from membership. Every group has a tendency to build up its own culture and to become self-contained.

The original model for Japanese groupism is to be found among the wet rice cultivators in northern Japan who developed a household system maintained through kinship, that added additional members who were considered quasi-kin to the household. The cohesion of the household depended upon the development of the shared sentiment that all household members were indispensable parts of the same whole. Rituals, ceremonies, and daily life itself served to reinforce this sentiment, creating sharp distinctions between household insiders and outsiders. Membership in a household acquired a high degree of selectivity.

In postwar Japan, business organizations in the modern culture of technology adopted the major features of the agrarian household model, a quasi-kinship social organization and cohesion based on shared sentiment. The vertical principle distributes the group members in numerous pairs within hierarchical networks. Each pair tries to establish a long-term relationship similar to that between parent and child. Intimacy (with no sexual connotation) is encouraged and highly admired. With some additional restrictions in membership such as academic achievements and gender distinction, groups in the mainstream culture of today's Japan are even more homogeneous and closed than the traditional agrarian model of northern Japan.

The rigidity and closedness of the Japanese group is imposed on its members through elaborate interaction rituals that bind each member to given pair relationships. The behavioral conditioning of the social process in rituals makes individuation of group members extremely difficult. Earlier, I pointed out the parallels between a revivalist religious group and secular contemporary Japanese groups, in order to emphasize that the essential characteristic of the group is that its members must submit to the "given" of the group, that is, to the ethos or collective sentiment already formed within the group. Such submission is accomplished through established interaction rituals that serve to condition both thought behavior and active behavior. Rituals are deliberately refined and occur with a spontaneity designed to puzzle newcomers to the group, who then must acculturate themselves by immersion in the group context. When group members master the interaction rituals, they are literally able to perceive each other's emotional states. Relationships become intimate, and the level of intelligibility of each other's actions is extremely sophisticated. This intimacy makes it difficult for members to relate to others functioning under a different ethos. Japanese groups are isolated from one another, competitive not internally but externally, concerned about the physical and psychological welfare of their members, but essentially indifferent to outsiders. It is a state akin to the concept of "corporate loyalty" taken to an extreme.

Because homogeneous group members are indifferent toward outsiders, the result has been the structural pluralism that is evident in Japanese society. The groupist culture creates a centrifugal momentum, resisting subordination to a greater whole than the group itself. To compensate for this pluralism, the Japanese government has tried to establish a set of unified groupist values, disseminating them through the educational system, under the rubric of nationalist spirit. However, the very quasi-kinship in the groupist organization is dependent on a "naturalism" in kinship relationships that insures the ideology of kinship but which is also frail. It requires constant attention and vigilance from its membership. This kind of naturalism promotes relationships that are more "natural than nature itself," and it relies upon cultural manipulation for sustenance. It is not easily imitated by the government's efforts to recreate it on a nationalistic level. Groupism is further threatened by the social environment, one of whose persistent features is individualism.

The government, in its efforts to promote nationalism, also faces the challenge of the postwar generation, who have reacted against the corporate loyalty ethic, wherein the Japanese company is a family rather than a community, by retreating into family-centrism. This tendency became distinctively visible toward the end of the 1980s, when the New Men began to privatize their groups. For them, the group no longer means one based on shared tasks or on identifying the group as one's family. Instead, groups are formed on the basis of voluntary, personal commitment. Family-centrism, only a vague social tendency in the 1960s, became the clear majority choice of the Japanese by the late 1980s. To the elders of Japan's modern culture of technology, this tendency indicates a withdrawal from social responsibility. In this book, I have called the withdrawal from corporate loyalty a form of *passive* individualism, because it is not an intentional rebellion against mainstream values. Its major significance is that it has emerged *within* the mainstream culture. It has led to finer differentiations between the kinds of groups found in the mainstream, accentuating the structural pluralism. It represents a further contribution to the momentum away from the centrism of Japanese society.

In contrast to the passive individualism identified in the mainstream, individualistic entrepreneurs on the periphery of Japanese society are actively trying to establish their own values. They deny the given authority, the status quo, and collectivist orientations; instead, they demonstrate independent decision-making, their own management styles, work enthusiasm (which they do not mind sharing as a value with the mainstream), private lifestyles, and even experimental marital relationships (quite unusual in contemporary Japan). The flourishing Japanese economy has provided such entrepreneurs with more opportunity than ever before to seek more competitive coexistence with giant corporations already established in the mainstream. In fact, the large companies need smaller manufacturers capable of adding more differentiation to mass-produced products, in order to meet the demands of the age for greater variety in smaller quantities. Entrepreneurs compete by creating associations with talented colleagues in complementary fields of specialization; these relationships are characterized by egalitarianism, and the associations themselves are an effort on the part of entrepreneurs to resist integration as mere subcontractors in the hierarchical order of the large corporations.

The increasing demand in Japan for internationalization has given individualistic entrepreneurs an advantageous position. Although Japan's economic dependence on foreign trade is actually much smaller than commonly assumed to be, there is an increasing demand for Japan to open its markets and to join the world economy. However, in contrast to Japan's earlier forays into the West, this tendency will not be characterized by Japan having to "Westernize" itself. On the contrary, it means that Japan will have to create its own ways to relate to people of different cultures. Individualists enjoy a distinct advantage over Ritual Men groupists in facing this challenge. As proof, those American business people doing business with the Japanese commonly assert that they are more at ease with entrepreneurs than with mainstream groupists, and they encourage the expansion of Japanese entrepreneurial ventures.

The relationship of individualistic entrepreneurs to the mainstream society may be seen either as complementary or as dialectical. In any case, Japanese individualists will no doubt stimulate their society toward the further development of its own modernity. As individualistic entrepreneurs, with their tremendous enthusiasm and high valuation of humanistic behavioral interaction—qualities not shared by the passive individualists in the mainstream—learn to respond more effectively to the demands of the international market, they will become a new vital force in Japan's future economy, and they may well be those who will lead Japan into true economic and cultural internationalization.

Bibliography

Asahi Newspaper Research Section. *Three Dimensional Research on the Japanese.* (in Japanese) Asahi Newspaper, 1988.

Befu, Harumi. *Japan: An Anthropological Introduction.* Tokyo: Charles E. Tuttle Company, 1971.

Benedict, Ruth. *The Chrysanthemum and the Sword.* Cleveland and New York: The World Publishing Company, 1969.

Bureau of Small and Intermediate Corporations. *Chusho Kigyo Yoran* (Guide to small and intermediate corporations). Tokyo: Chusho Kigyo Chosa Kai, 1989.

Burridge, Kennelm O. L. *Someone No One.* Princeton: Princeton University Press, 1979.

Central Labor Committee. *Rodojikan, Kyujitsu, Kyuka Chosa* (Work hours, holidays and vacation research). Tokyo: Roi Kyokai, 1987.

Doi, Takeo. *The Anatomy of Dependence.* New York: Harper and Row, 1973.

Dore, Ronald P. *City Life in Japan.* Berkeley and Los Angeles: University of California Press, 1958.

Drucker, Peter. "Behind Japan's Success." *Harvard Business Review,* (January–February 1981): 83–91.

Fukuda, Kenichi. *Uwayaku wa Naze Monowakari ga Waruika* (Why is your boss slow in understanding you?). Tokyo: Diamond Sha, 1977.

Fukutake, Tadashi. *Gendai Nihon Shakai Ron* (The theory of today's Japan). Tokyo: Tokyo University Press, 1972.

Goffman, Erving. *The Presentation of Self in Everyday Life.* Garden City, New York: Anchor Books, 1959.

———. *Interaction Ritual.* Garden City, New York: Anchor Books, 1967.

Hamaguchi, Eshun. *Kanjin-shugi no Shakai Nikon* (Japan, society of contextual men). Tokyo: Touyou Keizai, 1982.

Hayashi, et al. *Nihonjin no Kokuminsei* (National characteristics of the Japanese). No. 3. Tokyo: Idemitsu Shuppan, 1977.

Japan Future Society. *Nihongata High-tech-Shakai to Mirai* (Japanese style of high-tech society and the future). Tokyo: Kodan Sha, 1987.

Japan Management Association. *Dictionary of Everything about the Latest Statistics.* Tokyo: Japan Management Association, 1988.

Kamei, Hajime (ed.). *Gendai Yougo no Kiso Chishiki* (Basic Knowledge of Modern Terms.) Tokyo: Jiyuu Kokumin Sha, 1985.

Kim, Kyong-Dong. "The Distinctive Feature of South Korea's Development." In *In Search of an East Asian Development Model,* edited by Peter L. Berger and Hsin-Huang Michael Hsia, New Brunswick, New Jersey: Transaction Books, 1988, pp. 197–219.

Lewis, I. M. *Ecstatic Religion.* Middlesex, England: Penguin Books, 1971.

Ministry of Labor. *Rodo Tokei Yoran (Guide to Statistics Concerning Labor).* Tokyo: The Printing Bureau of the Ministry of Treasury, 1988.

Miyanaga, Kuniko. *Social Reproduction and Transcendence.* Ottawa: Canadian National Library (microfiche), 1983. Tokyo: Shikosha, 1983.

———. "Ritual Man: The Continuing Tradition in Human Relationships among the Youth." In *Perspectives on Contemporary Youth.* Tokyo: The United Nations University, pp. 177–192, 1988.

———. "Popularity of Robots in Japan." In *The ICU Journal of Social Science,* Tokyo: International Christian University, October 1985, pp. 111–123.

Morita, Akio. *Made in Japan.* New York: E. P. Dutton, 1986.

Moritani, Masanori. "New Division of Roles is Beginning between Smaller and Larger Businesses." *Gekkan Chusho Kigyo.* Tokyo: Diamond Sha, November 1987.

Munakata, Iwao. "The Distinctive Features of Japanese Development: Basic Cultural Patterns and Politico-Economic Processes." In *In Search of an East Asian Development Model,* edited by Peter L. Berger and Hsin-Huang Michael Hsia. New Brunswick, New Jersey: Transaction Books, Inc., 1988.

Nagai, Michio. *Dozoku.* Columbus, Ohio: The Ohio State University Research Foundation, 1953.

Nishioka, Mitsuaki. *Shikitari no Chie* (Wisdom in etiquette). Tokyo: Nihon Hourei, 1982.

NHK. *Portrait of the Family Today: Is the Household the Remaining Fortress?* (in Japanese) Tokyo: NHK Press, 1985.

Nobuhiro, Nagashima. "Nihonteki Shakai Kankei" (Japanese human relationships). In *Nihon-jin no Shakai (Society of the Japanese).* Tokyo: Kenkyu Sha, 1977.

Ogawa, Mario and Shuhei Kitade (eds.) *Encyclopedia of Everything: The Latest Edition* (in Japanese). Tokyo: Japan Management Association, 1988.

Otsuka, Yoshihiko. *Fashion Gyokai* (Fashion Business). Tokyo: Kyoika Sha, 1987.

Sengoku, Tamotsu. "Shinjinrui no Tanjo" (The birth of new men) and "Shinjinrui no Tokushitsu" (Special characteristics of new men). In *Shinjinrui ga Yatte-Kita (The Coming of New Men)*, edited by Shozo Ohgiya, Tokyo: PHP Kenkyusho, 1987, pp. 88–103, 104–135.

Shoko Chu kin Bank. *Gendai no Chu Sho Kigyo '87 (Today's Smaller Businesses, '87)*. Tokyo: Nihon Shoko Keizai Kenkyu Jo, 1987.

Small and Medium Enterprise Agency. *Chusho Kogyo Yoran (Guide to Small and Intermediate Businesses)*. Tokyo: Chusho Kigyo Chosa Kai, 1987.

Statistics Bureau of the Management and Coordination Agency of the Japanese Government. *Shugyo Kozo Kohon Chosa (Employment Structure Fundamental Research)*—quick print. Tokyo: 1988.

———. *Kokusai Tokei Yoran (Guide to International Statistics)*. Tokyo: 1987.

Tokyo Keizai Weekly. "Special Issue—The Age of Changing Occupations." Tokyo, 1987.

Tocqueville, Alexis de., *Democracy in America*. New York: Schocken Books, 1972.

Watanabe, Toshio. *Seicho no Ajia, Teitai no Ajia* (Asia in development, Asia in stagnation). Tokyo: Toyo Keizai Shimpo Sha, 1985.

White, Merry. *The Japanese Overseas: Can They Go Home Again?* New York: The Free Press, 1988.

Yamamoto, Kansai. *Kansai Kanzen Nensho* (Kansai, a perfect combustion). Tokyo: Shincho Bunko, 1983.

Yoneyama, Toshinao. *Nihonjin no Nakama Ishiki* (Group consciousness of the Japanese). Tokyo: Gendai Shinsho, Kodan Sha, 1976.

Index

135